WORD 365
FOR BEGINNERS

Peter John

TABLE OF CONTENT

INTRODUCTION

One of the most used applications in the Microsoft Office suite is Word. As Microsoft Office began to evolve with time, Word 365 came into the limelight.

Word 365 is one of the applications that came with Office 365. Word 365 is a widely used cloud-based software that is currently used by over a million companies in the world, because of its capabilities in executing office tasks with ease. In the year 2020, over 800,000 organizations in the US have subscribed to this package. The good news is, the numbers are tremendously increasing from time to time.

Word 365 does not in any way discard the traditional Word from being used from the time being memorial. However, Word 365 contains all the features in the traditional Word with a lot of upgrades that can never be found in the Word Offline irrespective of the version.

In case you are wondering why should you use Word 365 in your home, office, organization, etc, some of the following features will convince you

- Staying in sync with Office 365

- Streamlining your email

- Smart searching using the Smart Lookup

- Increased security

- Easy collaboration with other Microsoft users

- Mastering the keyboard shortcuts

- Saving and backing up files on OneDrive with ease

Having said these for you to hear, you don't want to miss what you have gotten to gain by exploring this user guide.

CHAPTER ONE

INTRODUCTION TO OFFICE 365

Before we begin to dive into Word 365 fully, we must have in-depth knowledge about Office 365.

Office 365 is a subscription-based version of the Microsoft Office Suite, which contains the same applications as the traditional versions of Office such as Word, Excel, PowerPoint, Outlook, OneNote, and depending on the plan subscribed to, you may get to use other applications and services such as Publisher, Planner, OneDrive, Exchange, SharePoint, Access, Skype, Yammer, and Microsoft Teams.

Office 365 which was launched in 2001, was the first cloud application of Microsoft Office and generates applications, services, and data hosted in Microsoft's servers.

Unlike the traditional Office Suite, Office 365 does not need to be installed for it to run. Also, Office 365 does not need any physical storage to store its information because it has an email hosting and a cloud storage space that allow the users to host their files online, and gain access to them, anytime and anywhere in as much they have an internet connection.

Why Should You Use Office 365?

There is no doubt that Office 365 and the traditional Office Suite have so many similarities. Despite all these similarities, Office 365 has some exclusive features that make it different from the traditional Office suite. However, these features are the major factors that will intrigue you to use Office 365. Now let us highlight them.

- **Easy Access from Anywhere:** Office 365 allows you to access your file anytime and anywhere using an internet connection, from any device. The Office 365 runs in a Microsoft data center, which allows the users to connect to the internet to access the software.
- **SharePoint**: One of the advantages of using Office 365 is that it allows you to use **SharePoint Online.** Using this service allows you to share and collaborate with others. To view the document by anyone in the organization, this service set up security permission.
- **Software Update:** Another advantage to the use of Office 365 is that it allows the users to get frequent software updates. These updates allow access to the latest features such as security updates, and bug fixes.
- **Secured Cloud Storage:** Office 365 has a secure working environment with high-security measures set in place such as two-factor authentication, which obstructs any authorized people to gain access to your files even while on your devices. With this in place, your confidential files are secured without any security threat or breach.
- **Improved Communication:** Office 365 comes with tools such as Skype, Yammer, Microsoft Teams, and Outlook, which help to enhance communication. For instance, Skype for Business allows you to hold conference calls and meetings with staff and external agencies anywhere in the world, regardless of the distance or location. Yammer, another tool for communication in Office 365 which serves as another form of social network used in an organization is used to post news feeds, email notifications, and create different channels for different purposes.

- **Automatic Upgrades**: Applications such as Word, Excel, Outlook, etc. are upgraded from time to time automatically at scheduled intervals. With this in place, the stress and cost involved in buying new software are removed as updates are included in the subscription for the Office 365 licenses.
- **Business Continuity:** Threats such as disasters and thefts cannot affect the flow of your business no matter what happens to your physical devices, emails, files, and data. This is because all files and data needed for workflow are saved and regularly backed up in Office 365 cloud.
- **Mix and Match Plans**: There are several different Office 365 subscription plans with different plans and features. Because of this, not everyone is going to need the same plan. Therefore, you can mix and match plans so that you will not need to pay above or below what you need.

Versions of Microsoft Office 365

There are several versions of Microsoft Office 365 of which you can choose to meet your demand and specifications.

- **Microsoft 365 Family:** This version of Microsoft Office 365 allows for 6 users at a time across unlimited PCs/Macs, tablets, and phones. The following are the features of the Microsoft 365 Family:

    - ✓ 1TB cloud storage per user for 6 users (6TB in total)
    - ✓ 60 minutes monthly Skype calls to mobile and landlines
    - ✓ Ongoing access to updates.
    - ✓ Includes Word, Excel, PowerPoint, OneNote, Outlook, Publisher (PC only), Access (PC only) OneDrive, Skype, Microsoft Teams.
    - ✓ Access to smart assistance features, with over hundreds of premium templates, photos, icons, and fonts in Word, Excel, and PowerPoint.

- ✓ Contact Support via chat or phone at no extra cost during the subscription.
- ✓ Save and share files across devices with OneDrive
- ✓ Experience advanced security protection in OneDrive and Outlook.
- ✓ 1-month free trial.
- ✓ Charges $ 99.99 per year and $9.99 per month

- **Microsoft 365 Personal:** This uses 1 PC/Mac across unlimited PCs/Macs, tablets, and phones and advanced security for all your devices. The following are the features of Microsoft 365 Personal

  - ✓ 1TB cloud storage per user for 1 user
  - ✓ 60 minutes monthly Skype calls for one user
  - ✓ Ongoing access to updates
  - ✓ Includes Word, Excel, PowerPoint, OneNote, Outlook, Publisher (PC only), Access (PC only) OneDrive, Skype, Microsoft Teams, Family Safety.
  - ✓ Saves and shares files across devices with OneDrive
  - ✓ Experience advanced security protection in OneDrive and Outlook.
  - ✓ Charges $ 69.99 per year and $6.99 per month

- **Microsoft Office 365 Education:** This version of Microsoft 365 is designed for students, teachers, university faculty, or staff. It has the following features
  - ✓ Sign up for free web access to Word, Excel, PowerPoint, OneNote, and Teams.
  - ✓ For students, it charges $2.50 and for teachers, it charges $2.85.
- **Microsoft 365 Business Standard:** The following are the features of Microsoft 365 Business Standard
  - ✓ Desktop versions of Offices apps such as Outlook, Word, Excel, PowerPoint, OneNote
  - ✓ Web versions of Word, Excel, PowerPoint.
  - ✓ Host email with a 50 GB mailbox and custom email domain.

- ✓ Creates a hub for teamwork with Microsoft Teams.
- ✓ 1TB cloud storage per user to store and share file
- ✓ Access to OneDrive, Exchange, Microsoft Teams, SharePoint, Yammer, Skype for Business.
- ✓ Uses one license to cover fully installed Office apps on five mobile devices, five tablets, and five PCs or Macs per user.
- ✓ Get help anytime and anywhere around the clock phone and web support from Microsoft.
- ✓ Charges 12.50 per month.

- **Microsoft 365 Business Premium:** The following are the features of Microsoft 365 Business Premium.

  - ✓ Desktop versions of Word, Excel. PowerPoint, OneNote, Outlook, Publisher, Access.
  - ✓ Web versions of Word, Excel, PowerPoint, Outlook
  - ✓ Allows up to 300 users
  - ✓ Access to OneDrive, Exchange, Microsoft Teams, SharePoint, Yammer, Skype for Business.
  - ✓ Stay up to date with the latest versions of Word, Excel, PowerPoint, and many more
  - ✓ Email hosting with 50GB mailbox and custom domain address.
  - ✓ Manages files from anywhere with 1TB of cloud storage on OneDrive per user.
  - ✓ Defends your business against advanced cyber threats with sophisticating phishing and ransomware protection.
  - ✓ Controls access to sensitive information making use of encryption to help keep data from being accidentally shared.
  - ✓ Secures or protects devices that connect your data and help keep iOS, Android, Windows, and Mac devices safe and up to date.

  - ✓ Charges $20 per month for each user
- **Microsoft 365 Business Basic:** The following are the features of Microsoft 365 Business Basis

- ✓ Host email with a 50GB mailbox and custom email domain address.
- ✓ A web version of Word, Excel, PowerPoint, Outlook, OneNote, Access, and Publisher.
- ✓ Stores and shares files with 1TB of OneDrive cloud storage per user.
- ✓ Host online meetings and video conferencing for up to 300 users.
- ✓ Get help anytime and anywhere around the clock phone and web support from Microsoft.
- ✓ Creates a hub for teamwork to connect your teams with Microsoft Teams.
- ✓ Video conferencing with up to 250 people.
- ✓ Charges $ 5 per month for each user.

- **Microsoft 365 Apps for Business:** The following are the features that coke with Microsoft 365 Apps for Business.

  - ✓ Web versions of Word, Excel, PowerPoint, Outlook, OneNote, and OneDrive.
  - ✓ Stores and shares files with 1TB of OneDrive cloud storage per user.
  - ✓ Allows up to 300 users
  - ✓ Automatically updates your apps with new features and capabilities every month.
  - ✓ Get help anytime and anywhere around the clock phone and web support from Microsoft.
  - ✓ Uses one license to cover fully installed Office apps on five mobile devices, five tablets, and five PCs or Macs per user.

  - ✓ Get help anytime and anywhere around the clock phone
  - ✓ Charges 8.25 per month for each user.

- **Microsoft 365 Apps for Enterprise (Office 365 ProPlan):** The following are the features of Office 365 ProPlus

- ✓ Desktop versions of Word, Excel, PowerPoint, OneNote, Access, and Publisher
- ✓ Web versions of Word, Excel, and PowerPoint.
- ✓ 1TB of OneDrive for file storage and sharing.
- ✓ Over 1,000 security and privacy controls, including custom permissions, password policies, and security groups.
- ✓ New features upgrades, quality patches, and security
- ✓ 5 PCs or Macs, 5 tablets and phones.
- ✓ Charges $19.14 per month

- **Office 365 Enterprise E1**: The following are the features of Office 365 Enterprise E1
  - ✓ Web versions of Word, Excel, and PowerPoint.
  - ✓ 1 TB of OneDrive file storage and sharing
  - ✓ 24/7 phone and web support.
  - ✓ 50 GB mailbox and custom email domain address.
  - ✓ Charges $8 per month for each user.
  - ✓ 5 PCs or Macs, 5 tablets and phones.

- **Office 365 Enterprise E3**: The following are the features of Office 365 Enterprise E3
  - ✓ Desktop versions of Word, Excel., PowerPoint, OneNote, Access, and Publisher.
  - ✓ Web versions of Word, Excel, and PowerPoint.
  - ✓ Unlimited personal cloud storage.
  - ✓ 24/7 phone and web support.
  - ✓ 100 GB mailbox and custom email domain address.
  - ✓ 5 PCs or Macs, 5 tablets and phones.
  - ✓ Charges $20.00 per month for each user.

- **Office 365 Enterprise E5:** The following are the features of Office 365 Enterprise E5
  - ✓ Desktop versions of Word, Excel., PowerPoint, OneNote, Access, and Publisher.
  - ✓ Web versions of Word, Excel, and PowerPoint.
  - ✓ Unlimited personal cloud storage.

  - ✓ 100 GB mailbox and custom email domain address.

- ✓ 5 PCs or Macs, 5 tablets and phones.
- ✓ 24/7 phone and web support.
- ✓ Charges $35.00 per month for each user.

CHAPTER TWO

GETTING STARTED WITH WORD 365

In the first chapter of this user guide, we have discussed explicitly Office 365, which serves as a foundation for the Office Suite apps, most importantly, word 365.

Having said all these, now let us fully go into Word 365.

What Is Word 365

Word 365 is a word processing application among all other applications in the Office 365 line of subscription services offered by Microsoft, to provide the users with the ability to create professional-quality documents, reports. Letters, and resumes and to add more dimensions to them, right on the web using a web browser, that is installed on the computer. Word 365 otherwise knowns as Word Online, uses cloud storage to save its file, and can only be accessed from a web browser on the computer system.

Versions of Microsoft Word

Before Word 365 came into existence, there are have been several versions of Microsoft Word being used. Quickly, we will be highlighting the versions of Microsoft Word up to date.

- **Word for Dos**: This is the first Microsoft Word to be released in 1983. It included graphics video mode and mouse support in a WYSIWYG. This version could operate the text mode or the graphical mode with just a slight difference. The Word for Doc has 6 versions ranging from 1.0 to 6.0. version
- **Word for Windows 1989 to 1995:** This is the first Windows, and it was released in November 1989 at the price of USD 498.
- **Word 95:** This was released as part of Office 95 and was tagged to be 7.0 dependably on all the Office components. This has only a few features running on the Win32 platform. However, the file format was not changed.
- **Word 97:** This is the version of Microsoft Word that introduced Visual Basic for Application (VBA) which is still in use up to today. Word 97 was the first copy of Word that uses Office Assistant. The Office Assistant was an animated help used in all Office programs.
- **Word 98:** This Windows version of Word was joined with Japanese/Korean Microsoft Office powered by Word 98 which could not be bought separately.
- **Word 2000:** Word 2000 was released together with Microsoft Office 2000 on March 29, 1999.
- **Word 2001/Word X:** Word 2001 was released in October 2000 and it was bundled with Macintosh Office with almost the same features of Word 2000.
- **Word 2002/XP:** This comes with Office XP which was released in 2001, containing many features as Word 2000 but a with a big difference called the Task Panes.
- **Word 2003:** Word 2003 comes with Office 2003 for the Windows operating system. This was released on August 19,

2003, and later for retail on October 21, 2003. This is the main successor of Office XP and the predecessor of Office 2007.

- **Word 2004:** Word 2004 has no new changes made to it. The Macintosh version of Office was released in May 2004 while the Windows version was a substantial cleanup of the various Office applications such as Word, Excel, PowerPoint.

- **Word 2007:** Word 2007 contains a lot of upgraded changes such as a new XML-base file format, an integrated equation edited, a redesigned interface, and bibliographic management. Word 2007 uses a new file format called Docx. This was released on January 30, 2007.

- **Word 2008:** The Word 2008 was released on January 15, 2008, with most of its features from Word 2007.

- **Word 2010**: Word 2010 is the successor of Word 2007 and the predecessor of Office 2013. This version of Word was released for manufacturing on April 15, 2010, it became available for retail and online purchase on June 15, 2008.

- **Word 2011**: The version available for Word 2011 is the Mac version.

- **Word 2013:** The Word 2013 released on January 29, 2013, focused more on Cloud computing with the ability to get your documents saved on OneDrive. This was later replaced by Word 2016.

- **Word 2016:** Word 2016 was released on July 9, 2016. This is an improved version of Word 2013.

- **Word 2019:** Another version that replaced Word 2016 is Word 2019. This contains upgraded features such as Sign in, Share, Auto-resume, etc. This was finally replaced by Word 365.

- **Word 365:** Word 365 was released on September 24. 2011 is a word processing application among all other applications in the Office 365 line of subscription services offered by Microsoft, to provide the users with the ability to create professional-quality documents, reports. Letters, and resumes and to add more dimensions to them, right on the web using a web browser, that is installed on the computer. This version of Word includes features such as speech dictation, resume assistant, sharing of documents online, etc.

Word 365 System Requirement on Windows and Macs

To use Word 365 on your device, be it Windows or Mac, you need to have a sound understanding of the system requirement.

Below are the system requirements to run Word 365 on your Windows or Mac devices.

Microsoft 365 Plans for Home Subscription

COMPONENT REQUIREMENT	WINDOWS (OS)	MACKINTOSH (OS)
Computer and processor	1.6 GHz or faster, 2 core	Intel Processor
Memory	4 GB RAM; 2 GB RAM (32-bit)	4 GB RAM
Hard disk	4 GB of available disk space	10 GB of available disk space
Display	1280 x 768 screen resolution (32-bit requires hardware acceleration for 4K and higher)	1280 x 800 resolution.
Graphics	Graphics hardware acceleration requires DirectX 9 or later, with WDDm 2.0 or higher for Windows 10 or WDDm 1.3 or higher for Windows 10 Fall Creators Update)	No graphics requirement.

Operating System	Windows 10 SAC, Window 8.1, Window Server 2019, or Windows Server 2016.	The new version of the macOS and the previous two versions.
Browser	The current version of Microsoft Edge, Internet Explorer, Safari, Chrome, or Firefox	The current version Microsoft Edge, Internet Explorer, Safari, Chrome, or Firefox
.NET Version	Some features need .NET 3.5 or 4.6 and higher to also be installed.	None
Other	Strong internet connection	Strong internet connection

Microsoft 365 Plans for Business, Education, and government

COMPONENT REQUIREMENT	WINDOWS (OS)	MACKINTOSH (OS)
Computer and processor	1.6 GHz or faster, 2-core. 2 GHz or greater recommended for Skype for Business.	Intel Processor
Memory	4 GB RAM; 2 GB RAM (32-bit)	4 GB RAM
Hard disk	4 GB of available disk space	10 GB of available disk space
Display	1280 x 768 screen resolution (32-bit requires hardware acceleration for 4K and higher)	1280 x 800 resolution.

Graphics	Graphics hardware acceleration requires DirectX 9 or later, with WDDm 2.0 or higher for Windows 10 or WDDM 1.3 or higher for Windows 10 Fall Creators Update). Skype for Business needs DirectX 9 or later, 128 MB graphics memory, and 32-bits-per-pixel-capable format.	No graphics requirement.
Operating System	Windows 10 SAC, Window 8.1, Window Server 2019, or Windows Server 2016.	The new version of the macOS and the previous two versions.
Browser	The current version of Microsoft Edge, Internet Explorer, Safari, Chrome, or Firefox	The current version Microsoft Edge, Internet Explorer, Safari, Chrome, or Firefox
.NET Version	Some features need .NET 3.5 or 4.6 and higher to also be installed. Microsoft Teams requires 4.6 or higher.	None
Other	Strong internet connection	Strong internet connection

Video calls and meetings	2.0 GHz processor and 4.0 GB RAM or higher.	2.0 GHz processor and 4.0 GB RAM or higher
Team live event	Core i5 Kaby Lake processor, 4.0 GB RAM or higher	4.0 GB RAM or higher

Becoming A Microsoft User

Before you can use Word 365, you must first have an account with Microsoft. Without this account, there is no way you can use Word 365 in Office 365. To create an account with Microsoft, follow the steps given below

- Go to the **Microsoft Office Website** from your browser https://www.office.com
- When the page is open, click on **Get Office**

Welcome to Office

Your place to create, communicate, collaborate, and get great work done.

- On this page, there are two options to select: For **Home and For Business.** Select any of the options and click on **Buy Now**

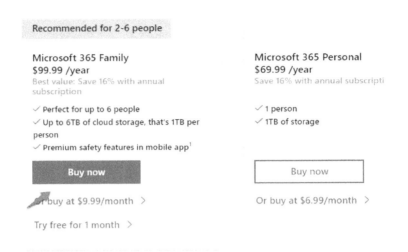

- A sign-in window pops. You can sign in and if you do not have an account, click on **Create one**

- Create an account by either entering an e-mail address or phone number by clicking on **Use a phone number instead** and enter the phone number. Then click on **Next.**
- Enter your password in the Show password option, and then click on **Next**.
- Fill in the bio data as displayed on the page and then click on **Next.**

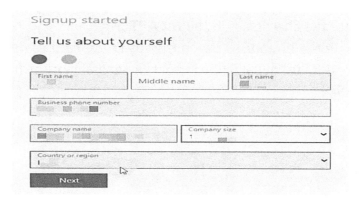

- Microsoft will request to send a verification code to your e-mail or phone number, click on **Send Verification Code**. When you receive the verification code, enter it in the verification box, and then click on **Verify**

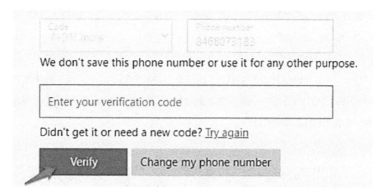

- On this page, enter your username, password and re-enter your password. Select the box asking if you want information, tip, and offer. Then click on **Sign in**

- Input the characters in the **reCAPTCHA**
- Select the options to pay: either by credit card or debit card, bank account, or PayPal. Then input the necessary information and click on **Save.**

- Select or deselect the box asking if you want promotional e-mails from Microsoft. Then click on **Subscribe.**
- Once the payment is successful, you will be directed to your Office 365 dashboard, where you install Office by following the instructions given.
- After you are done with these processes, click on **Next.**
- Finally, you can now access the programs in Office 365 by clicking on the **Start menu**

Exploring Word 365 Screen Interface

Word 365 has the same screen interface as the traditional Word (2010, 2013, 2016, and 2019). The only difference here is that; Word 365 is used within the web browser.

Here in this session, we will be explaining the features that come with Word 365. These features will be based on the Title bar and the Menu bar.

The Title Bar

The Title bar is what displays the name of the current document that is being worked on. The Title bar is located at the top of the screen interface. At the top of the screen, the name of the document is displayed e.g. Document 1 as shown in the image below

Navigating Through the Menu Bar

The Menu bar is located directly below the Title bar. The Menu bar is what contains all the tabs needed to work on Word 365. The Menu bar begins with the File tab and ends with the Help tab.

Now let us go through each tab on the Menu bar, see their functions and how they are used.

File Tab

The File tab is the first tab to see when you go to the Menu bar. When you click on the File tab, the following features are displayed

- **Home:** When you click on Home under the File tab, you get to see the following features
  - **New:** This option allows you to open a new document.
  - **Open:** This option allows you to open a previously saved document.

- **Info:** This option provides additional information about the document you have worked on such as size, pages, words, total editing, title, tags, and much more info about the documents. This option also allows you to protect your document, restricting editing, and check for issues.

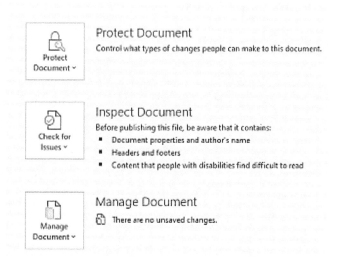

- **Save:** This option allows you to save the active document with its current file name, location, and format.
- **Save As:** This option allows you to save by opening a window that allows you to change the file name, location, and format.

- **Print:** This option allows you to print the active and allows you to change the print options.

- **Share:** With this option, you can share your documents with others online via emails, blogs, or websites.

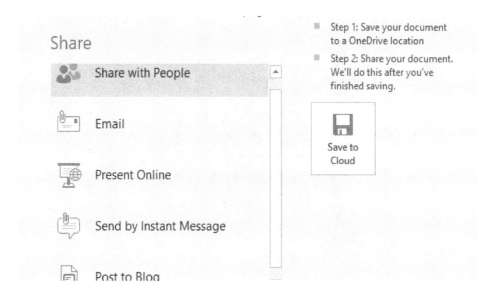

- **Export:** The Export option allows you to transfer a file from Word into another Office 365 app such as PowerPoint, Excel, etc. by changing the file formats.

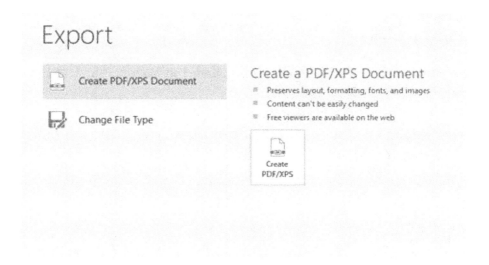

- **Transform:** This allows you to transform your documents into a web page.

- **Close:** This allows you to close the document you are working on.

Home Tab

The Home tab is the default tab displayed in Word 365. The Home tab contains the following features.

- **Clipboard**: The clipboard ribbon allows you to use the options stated below

- o **Cut**: to remove a selected portion of the document and save it into the clipboard.
- o **Copy**: To make another copy of a document and then save it on the clipboard.
- o **Format painter**: This allows you to duplicate a text format into another text format
- o **Paste**: This tool Is what produced or displayed the items cut or copied to the right location.
- **Font Ribbon Tab:** The Font ribbon contains tools for modifying the fonts in the Word 365 document. With Font ribbon, you can do the following.

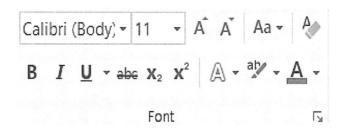

- o **Bold:** To make the selected texts bold in the word documents.
- o **Italics:** To make selected texts in the word document slant or slope.
- o **Underline:** To underline the selected texts in a Word document.
- o **Strikethrough:** To cut a line across the selected texts in the Word document
- o **Font Style:** This option allows you to change your text style to the one you desire.
- o **Font Size:** This is used to adjust the font size of a text.
- o **Font Color:** This is used to change to font color of your texts.
- o **Text Highlighted Color:** This is used to change the background of the selected texts.
- o **Subscript:** This is used to type letters or texts below the line.

o **Superscript:** This is used to type letters or texts above the line.
o **Text Effect and Typography:** This option allows you to add some flairs to your texts by applying texts effects such as shadow or glow.
o **Change Case:** This is used to change the selected texts to uppercase, lowercase, or other common capitalization.
o **Clear Formatting:** This is used to remove all the formatting in the texts selected, and leaving the normal text unformatted.

- **Paragraph Ribbon Tab:** The Paragraph tab allows you to adjust the paragraphs in your texts by applying the paragraphs editing formats such as bullets, numbering, alignments, etc. listed below

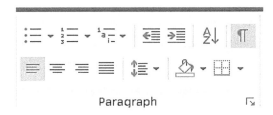

Paragraph

o **Bullet:** This is used to create a bullet list using the bullet list format in the bullet library.

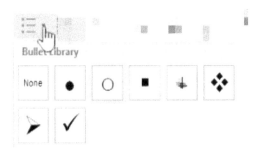

o **Numbering:** This is used to create a numbering list using the numbering list format in the numbering library.]

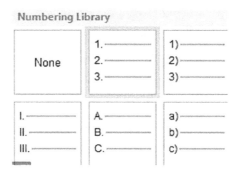

- **Multilevel List**: This is used to create a multilevel list to organize an item or create an outline. This is a mixture of both the bullet and numbering listing.

- **Align Left**: This is used to align your texts to the left margin
- **Center**: This is used to place your content at the center
- **Align Right**: This is used to align your texts to the left margin
- **Justify:** To evenly place the content in the left and margin

- **Decrease and Increase Indent**: This option allows you to move the paragraph closer or farther away from the margin

- o **Line and Paragraph Spacing:** This is used to set how space appears between lines of texts or between paragraphs

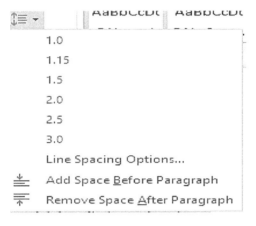

- o **Sort**: This arranges the current selection in alphabetical or numerical order.

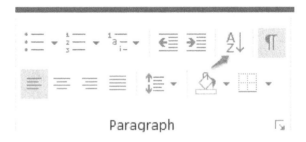

- o **Shading**: This is used to change the color behind the selected texts, paragraphs, or tables.

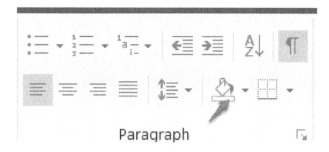

- o **Borders**: This option allows you to add or remove borders from your selection. '

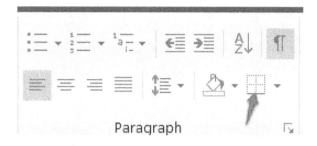

- **Styles:** This is a set of formatting characteristics that can be applied to your tables, texts, and list of your documents to change their appearance.

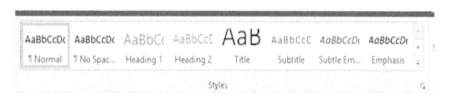

- **Editing:** The Editing tool allows you to find, replace, and select texts in the documents.

- **Dictate:** This is a new tool in Word 365 that allows you to use speech to type rather than using the keyboard.

Dictate

Voice

Insert Tab

The Insert tab as the name implies, allows you to insert interesting features to your content on Word 365. The following are the tools in the Insert tab:

- **The Page Ribbon:** The Page ribbon when clicked on, pops the following;
  - o **Cover Page:** This is the drop-down that contains commands such as Built-in, Remove Current Cover Page, and Save Selection to Cover Page Gallery.
  - o **Blank Page:** This option allows you to insert two-page breaks into the document; one above the current insertion point and another one below it.
  - o **Page Break:** This allows you to insert the page break instead of displaying the Breaks dialog box.

- **Tables:** This option allows you to insert tables of different sizes and shapes into your content.

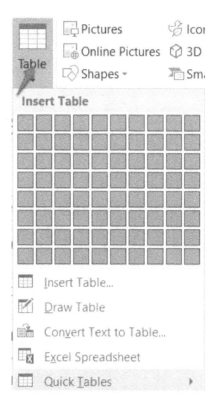

- **Illustration Ribbon:** This option allows you to insert features such as Pictures, Online Pictures, Shapes, Icons, 3D Models, SmartArt, Charts, and screenshots into your documents.

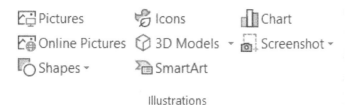

Illustrations

- **Add-ins Ribbon Tab:** With this feature, Microsoft users can merge external application features with Word 365.

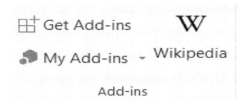

Add-ins

- o **Media Ribbon Tab:** With this feature, you can insert online video into your content.

- o **Link Ribbon Tab:** With this feature, you can link creations into other files, webpage, cross-references, etc.

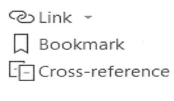

- **Comment Ribbon Tab:** This allows you to add a note about a part of a document.

- **Header & Footer:** This allows you to insert header, footer, and page number to your document.

Header & Footer

- **Text Ribbon**: This allows you to insert features such as Text Box, Quick Parts, Drop Cap, Signature, etc.

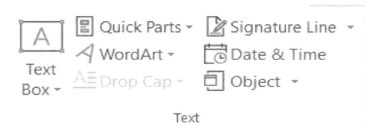

Text

Symbol Ribbon: With this option, you can insert equations and symbols into your documents.

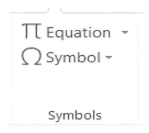

Symbols

Draw Tab

The Draw tab is only available in Word 365. The Draw tab allows you to add notes, create shapes, edit texts, and lots more. The draw tab offers the three types of drawing textures; pen, pencil, and highlighter.

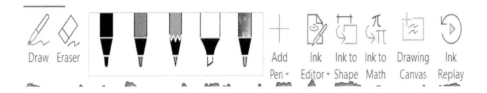

Design Tab

The Design tab is primarily focused on applying Themes and Quick Styles Texts to your documents. The following are the features in the Design tab

- **Document Formatting:** When you go to this ribbon, you get to use the following features.

Document Formatting

- o **Themes**: This contains a drop-down list of themes that can be applied to your documents. The drop-down list contains commands such as Built-in, More Themes on Microsoft Office Online, Browse for Themes, and Save Current Themes.

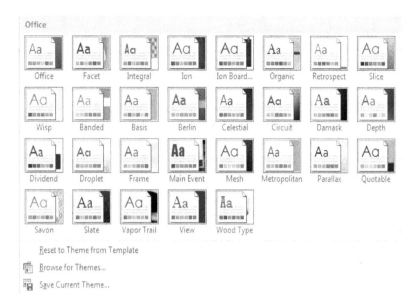

- Style Set: This option allows you to change the look of your document by selecting a new style layer. The Style Set affects the font and paragraphs of your document.

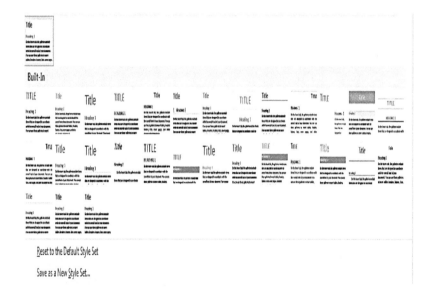

- Colors: This option displays the list of all the colors available and allows you to change the color component of the active theme.

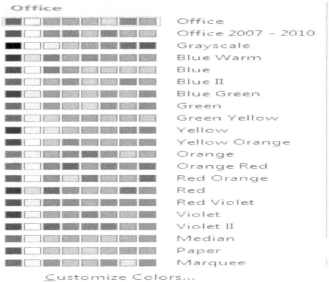

- o **Font**: This displays a list of all the fonts available and allows you to change the font components of the active theme.

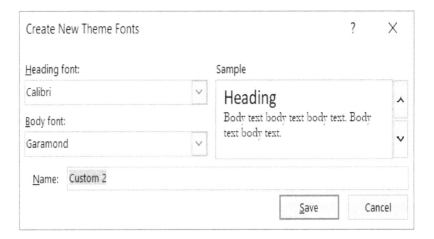

- o **Paragraph Spacing:** This option allows you to change the line and paragraphs spacing of your documents. This contains commands such as No Paragraph Space, Compact, Tight, Open, Relaxed, Double, Custom Paragraph Spacing.
- o **Effect:** This displays a list of all the available effects and changes the components of the active theme.

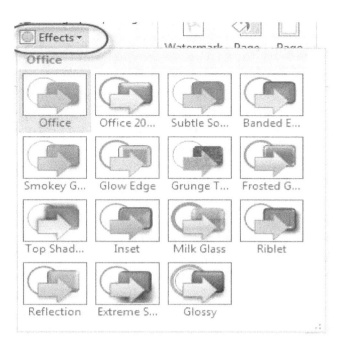

- Set as Default: This allows you to use the current look for all the documents.

- **Page Background:** The Page Background ribbon has the following features:

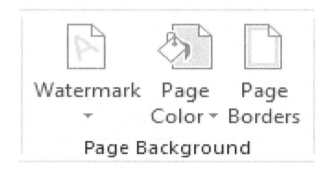

- **Watermark:** This is a tool used to design the background of a document, using either text or an image. The Watermark dropdown contains the following commands: Custom Watermark, Remove Watermark, and Save Selection to Watermark Gallery.

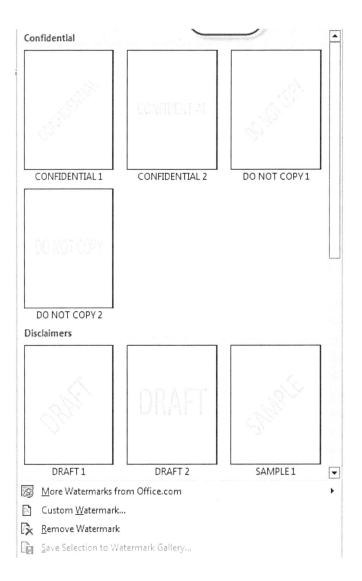

Confidential

CONFIDENTIAL 1   CONFIDENTIAL 2   DO NOT COPY 1

DO NOT COPY 2

Disclaimers

DRAFT 1   DRAFT 2   SAMPLE 1

- More Watermarks from Office.com ►
- Custom Watermark...
- Remove Watermark
- Save Selection to Watermark Gallery...

- o **Page Color:** This option allows you to change the background color of your page and displays the full theme color palette.
- o **Page Borders:** This option displays the Border and Shading dialog box.

Layout Tab

The layout tab offers tools needed for page setup, paragraph indent, and spacing options. The following are the tools available in the layout tab:

- **Page Setup:** This is where you display the Page Setup dialog box and the Margin dialog box

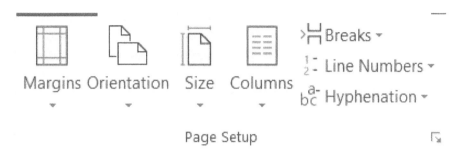

- o **Margins:** This is where you set your margin by either choosing from the built-in margin settings or customize your margin.
- o **Orientation:** This is where you change the orientation of your current document to either Portrait or landscape.
- o **Size:** This is where you get to select the paper size from the available paper sizes.
- o **Columns:** This is where you split your documents into two or more columns.
- o **Breaks:** This allows you to select from the drop-down list commands such as Page Break, Remove Page Break and Reset All Page Breaks.
- o **Line Numbers:** Here you get to select from the drop-down list commands such as None, Continuous, Restart Each Page, Restart Each Section, etc.
- o **Hyphenation:** This option moves your texts to the next line when it exceeds the space given. This option contains command such as None. Automatic, Manual, and Hyphenation Options.
- **Paragraph:** This displays the Paragraph dialog box, Indent, and Spacing tab.

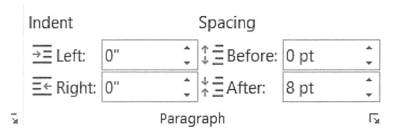

- o **Indent**: This option determines how much indentation is to be applied to the paragraph of the current selection in the document, whether to the left or right.
- o **Spacing**: This option determines how much spacing is to be applied to the paragraph of the current selection in the document, whether to the left or right.

- **Arrange:** The Arrange group contains the following features.

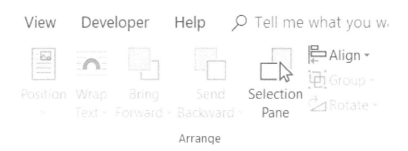

- o **Position**: This option displays how pictures can be positioned in a document such as Line With Text and Text Wrapping.\
- o **Wrap Text**: This option determines how texts wrap around objects, and it consists of the following commands: In Line with Text, Square, Tight, Through, etc.
- o **Bring Forward**: This option brings the selected object forward one level so that it is hidden behind fewer objects.
- o **Send Backward**: This option brings the selected object back one level so that it is hidden behind more objects.
- o **Selection Pane**: This displays the list of all your objects. With this option, you can select the objects, change the order, and show visibility.

- Align: This allows you to change the placements of your selected objects in the documents.
- Group: This allows you to join objects together, move and format them as if they were a single object.
- Rotate: This option allows you to rotate or flip the selected objects.

Reference Tab

The Reference tab gives you the access to use all the commands used for creating references in your documents. The following are the commands available in the Reference tab

- **Table of Contents:** The following features are found in the Table of content group

Table of Contents

- **Table of Content:** This option gives you an outline of your document by inserting a table of content. The drop-down contains such as Built-in, Insert Table of Content, and Save Selection to Table of Contents Gallery.
- **Add Text:** This helps to add the current heading in the Table of content.
- **Update Table:** This option allows you to refresh the table of contents so that all entries are referred to the correct page number.

- **Footnotes:** With this, you can display the Footnote and Endnote dialog box. The following are the features available in the Footnotes group

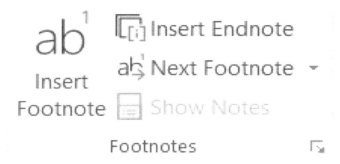

Footnotes

- o **Insert Footnote:** This option allows you to provide information about anything in your document by adding a note on the current page of the document.
- o **Insert Endnote:** This allows you to add notes such as comments and citations to provide more information about something at the end of the document.
- o **Next Footnote:** With this option, you can jump to the next footnote.
- o **Show Notes:** This shows where the footnotes and endnotes are in the documents.

- **Research:** The following are the features in the Research group:

Research

- o **Smart Lookup:** This allows you to definitions, images, web pages, and other results from different online sources.

- **Citations and Bibliography:** The following are the features in Citations and Bibliography.

Citations & Bibliography

- o **Insert Citation**; This allows you to refer to a source of information by citing the book, articles, or other materials it comes from.
- o **Manage Source**: This organizes the sources cited in your document.
- o **Style:** This allows you to choose the style of your citations in the documents.
- o **Bibliography:** This makes a list of your sources in a bibliography or a work cited section.

- **Captions:** The following are the features in the Caption group

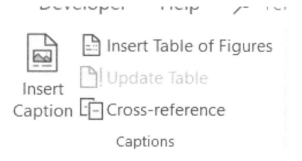

Captions

- o **Insert Caption:** This allows you to insert or add a caption below a picture or graphics to give a short description.
- o **Insert Table of Figures:** To insert a list of captioned objects and their page numbers for quick reference.
- o **Update Table:** To update the table of figures to include all the entries in the documents.

- o **Cross-reference:** To refer to specific places in your document such as headings, figures, and tables.
- **Index:** The following are the features in the Index group

Index

- o **Mark Entry:** This is used to mark the selected texts to the index in the documents.
- o **Insert Index:** This is used to add or insert index listing keywords and page numbers they appear on.
- o **Update Index:** This is used to update the index so that all the entries refer to the correct page number.

- **Table of Authorities:** The following are the features of the Table of Authorities group:

Table of Authorities

- o **Mark Citation:** This is used to add the selected texts to the Table of Authority.
- o **Insert Table of Authorities:** This is used to insert or add a table of authorities for cases, statutes, and other authorities cited in the documents.
- o **Update Table:** This is used to update the table of authorities to add all the citations.

Mailings Tab

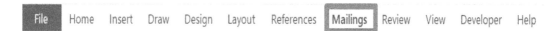

This tab is responsible for finalizing a successful mail range. The following are the features under the Mailing tab.

- **Create:** The Create group is focused on creating envelopes and labels.

- o **Envelopes:** This allows you to create and print envelopes in different sizes. You can also format the address and add electronic postage to it.
- o **Labels:** This also allows you to create and print labels in different sizes.

- **Start Mail Merge**: The Start Mail Merge group is specifically designed with tools that help merge your mails. The following are the tools or features in the Start Mail Merge group:

- o **Start Mail Merge:** This is used to create a document you intend to send to multiple people. The drop-down contains command such as Letters, E-mail messages, Envelopes, etc.
- o **Select Recipients:** This option allows you to select the list of people you intend to send your documents to. You can type a new list, select an existing one, or choose from Outlook contact.
- o **Edit Recipient Lists:** This allows you to make changes to your recipient lists or select a certain set of people to get the mails. With this option, you can also sort, filter, find, and remove the duplicate, and validate addresses on the list.
- • **Write & Insert Field:** The Write & Insert Field group commands are only accessible when you are in Mail Merge documents. The following are the features in this group:

- o **Highlight Merge Fields:** This is used to highlight the field in your documents. With this option, you easily identify where contents from your recipient list will be inserted.
- o **Address Block:** This allows you to add an address to your letter. You can also indicate the format and location of the list
- o **Greeting Line:** This allows you to add a greeting to your documents.
- o **Insert Merge Field:** This helps you to add a field from a recipient list to the documents. Such fields include Last Name, Home Phone, and Company Name.
- o **Rules:** This allows you to add rules such as Ask, If, Then, etc. to the mail merge.
- o **Match Field:** This allows you to match the required field with the recipient list.
- o **Update Labels:** This updates all the labels in the document to correspond with the information from the recipient list.

- **Preview Result:** The following are the features of the Preview Results group:

- o **Preview Results**: This is used to insert data from your recipient list to the merged field. This option cannot work when there is no field in the documents.
- o **First Record**: This is used to view the first record in the recipient list.
- o **Previous Record**: This is used to view the previous record in the recipient list.
- o **Go to Record**: This is used to view a specific record in the recipient list.
- o **Next Record**: This is used to view the next record in the recipient list.
- o **Last Record:** This is used to view the last record in the recipient list.
- o **Find Recipient:** This is used to find a specific recipient and locate the recipient document to view.
- o **Check Errors:** This option tells Word 365 how to deal with errors that occur during mail merge. This also checks for errors in the mail merge.
- **Finish:** This group only has one feature;

- o **Finish & Merge:** This allows you to choose how you want to finalize the mail merge either by opening the mail in a new window, sending the mail to the printer, or sending via email.

Review Tab

The Review tab is designed to give detailed information about the documents you are working on. The following are the features in the Review tab.

- **Proofing**: The following tools are used for proofing your documents.

Proofing

- o **Spelling & Grammar:** This allows you to check the spelling and grammar errors in your document.
- o **Thesaurus:** This is a research service that suggests saying what you mean in another way.
- o **Word Count:** This counts the words, characters, and lines in a document.
- **Accessibility:**
  - o **Check Accessibility**: ensure that your file follows accessibility practices.

Check Accessibility

Accessibility

- **Language:** The following are the features in the Language group

- o **Translate:** This helps to translate text into different languages by using bilingual dictionaries and online services.
- o **Language:** This helps to choose the language for proofing tools such as spelling checks.

- **Comments:** The following are the features of the Comments group.

- o **New Comment:** This adds or inserts a note to the active cell selection.
- o **Delete:** This is used to delete selected comments in the active selection.
- o **Previous:** To move to the previous comment.
- o **Next:** To move to the next comment
- o **Show Comments:** To view all the comments in the documents.
- **Tracking:** The following are the features of the Tracking group;

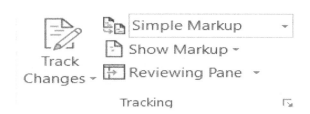

- o **Track Changes:** This allows you to keep track of changes that occur in the documents.
- o **Display for Review:** This contains the drop-down commands on how you like to see changes in your document.
- o **Show Markup:** This option allows you to choose the types of markup to display in your documents.
- o **Receiving Panel:** This displays all the changes made to your documents in a list.

- **Changes:** The following are the features in the Changes group

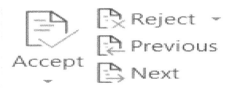

Changes

- o **Accept:** This accepts the change tracked and then moves to the next one.
- o **Reject**: This undo the change tracked and then moves to the next one.
- o **Previous:** This moves to the previous tracked change
- o **Next:** This moves to the next tracked change

- **Compare:** The Compare group contains the following feature
  - o **Compare:** This is used to compare two documents to see the similarities between them. Also, with this option, you can combine revisions from many authors to form a single document.

Compare

Compare

- **Protect**: The Protect group contains the following features:

Protect

- ○ **Block Authors:** This option prevents others from making changes to the texts selected in the document
- ○ **Restrict Editing:** This option sets boundaries on how others can make changes to the documents.
- **Resume:** The Resume group has just a feature which is highlighted below

Resume

- ○ **Resume Assistant:** This allows the users to get different templates.

View Tab

The View tab contains the feature to preview content, read content, zoom in and out, etc. The following are the features in the View tab.

- **Views:** The Views group contains commands that allow you to view your document in different ways.

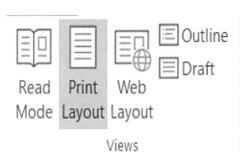

Views

- **Read Mode:** This option is also referred to as Full-Screen Reading. This allows you to maximize the Word window on the screen, in such a way that all the toolbars are removed for easy reading of the documents.
- **Print Layout:** This displays the document the way it should be when printed out. This is the default view.
- **Web Layout:** This displays the document the way it should appear on the web page.
- **Outline:** This displays the document in the outline where content is displayed in a bulleted form.
- **Draft:** This displays the document in draft mode for easy and quick editing. When the document is displayed in this mode, the headers and footers are not visible to see.
- **Immersive:** This Immersive group has just one feature which is highlighted below.
  - **Learning Tool:** This is a tool that uses proven techniques to advance reading for people not minding their age and ability.

Learning Tools

Immersive

- **Show:** The following are the features in the Show group

☐ Ruler
☐ Gridlines
☐ Navigation Pane

Show

- o **Ruler:** This is used to display a ruler next to your documents.
- o **Gridlines:** This is used to display gridlines in the background of your document for perfect object replacement.
- o **Navigation Pane**: This option allows you to move around your document with ease.
- **Zoom:** The Zoom group is concerned about adjusting the display percentage of the active document. The following commands are found in the Zoom group:

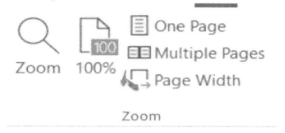

Zoom

- o **Zoom:** This tool allows you to zoom your document to the size you want.
- o **100%:** This allows you to zoom your document to 100%.
- o **One Page:** This allows you to zoom an entire page of your document to fit in the application window.
- o **Two Pages:** This allows you to zoom the two pages of your documents to fit in the application window.
- o **Page Width**: This allows you to zoom the width of the page to match the width of the application window.

- **Window:** The Window group contains the following features:

Window

- o **New Window:** This allows you to open a new window of the active documents.
- o **Arrange All:** This stacks your open windows side by side on the screen so that you can see them all at once.
- o **Split:** This divides the current window into two parts.
- o **View Side by Side:** This allows you to display two documents side by side so that they can be easily compared, rather than switching back and forth between the documents.
- o **Synchronous Scrolling:** This option allows you to compare two documents line by line, or scan for differences. Here you get to view two documents side by side.
- o **Reset Window Position:** This option allows you to reset the position of the window so that the two documents displayed side by side are occupying the same level of space.
- o **Switch Windows:** This allows you to switch between another open window.
- **Macros:** The Macros group only has one feature and it is highlighted below
  - o **Macros:** This is used to view, record, or pause macro. You can also use this button to view the list of macros

Macros

- **SharePoint**: The SharePoint group has one feature and it is highlighted below:

- **Properties**: This works automatically with contents or documents in SharePoint Online and OneDrive for Business libraries.

Developer Tab

The Developer tab includes additional commands relating to macros and Visual Basic. The following are the features in the Developer tab.

- Code: The following are the features in the Code group

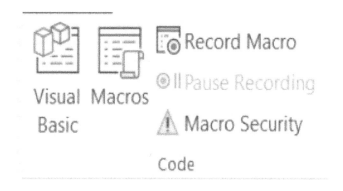

- **Visual Basic**: This is used to open the Visual Basic Editor which is used to create and edit the VBA macros.
- **Macros**: This shows the list of macros you can work with. Here you can run, edit, and delete macros.

- o **Record Macro:** This is used to start or stop recording a macro. This is used to pause the macro recording.
- o **Macro Security:** This is used to customize the Macro security settings.
- **Add-ins**: The Add-ins group contain the following features:

Add-ins

- o **Add-ins:** This allows you to insert Add-ins and use the web to improve your work.
- o **Word Add-Ins:** This option allows you to manage the add-ins available for use with the file.
- o **COM Add-Ins:** This allows you to manage the available COM add-ins.
- **Controls:** The following features are found in the Control group:

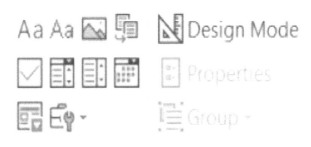

Controls

- o **Rich Text**: This button allows you to insert rich text content control.
- o **Plain Text**: This button allows you to insert plain content control.

- o **Picture**: This button allows you to insert picture content control.
- o **Building Block Gallery:** This button allows you to insert building block gallery content control.
- o **Check Box:** This button allows you to insert check box content control.
- o **Combo Box:** This button allows you to insert combo box content control.
- o **Drop Down Box:** This button allows you to insert drop-down box content control.
- o **Date Picker:** This button allows you to insert date content control.
- o **Repeating Section:** This button allows you to insert content control that contains other controls and repeats the content of the controls as needed.
- o **Legacy Tool:** This button allows you to insert ActiveX control or form control.
- o **Design Mode**: This allows you to turn off or on the design mode.
- o **Control Properties:** This allows you to view or modify the properties of the selected control.
- o **Group:** This allows you to group or ungrouped a selected text.
- • **Mapping:** The Mapping group has one feature and it is highlighted below:

XML Mapping
Pane

Mapping

- o **XML Mapping Pane**: This is where the XML data is stored and create content controls that are linked to it in the document.

- **Protect**: The Protect group contains the following features:

- o **Block Authors:** This option prevents others from making changes to the texts selected in the document
- o **Restrict Editing:** This option set boundaries on how others can make changes to the documents.
- **Template:** The Template group has just a feature which is highlighted below

- o **Document Template:** This allows users to view and change the attached document templates and also manage the global template and ads-ins.

Help Tab

The Help tab is a newly added feature in Word 365 that offers a solution, contact support, and feedback to Microsoft users. This tab provides fast access to the Help Task Pane and some useful website links.

- **Help & Support:** The following are the features in the Help & Support group:

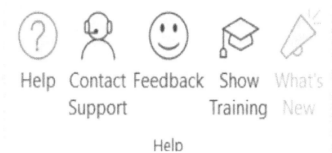

- o **Help:** This allows you to display the Help task pane showing the home page. You can also display this option by pressing F1.
- o **Contact Support:** This allows you to display the Help task pane asking for help.
- o **Feedback:** This displays the Feedback tab from the File tab.
- o **Showing Training:** This displays the Help task pane showing the training videos.
- o **What's New**: This shows the most recently installed updates. You can also access this from the File tab and Account.

CHAPTER THREE

USING SPEED TECHNIQUES WHILE WORKING WITH WORD

This chapter is focused on using shortcuts and commands that will improve your speed while using Word 365.

In the previous chapter, we have discussed everything you need to know about the screen interface and the tabs associated with it. Here in this session, we will be going deeper on how to speedily work with the documents.

Creating a New Document

The document is the umbrella where items such as letters, memos, newsletters, calendars, resumes, etc are categorized under Word. To create a document om Word 365, follow the steps giving below

- On the **Menu bar**, go to the **File tab** and click on **New**
- Select **Blank Document**
- Then click on **Create button** in the preview window; here the new document is displayed on the screen.

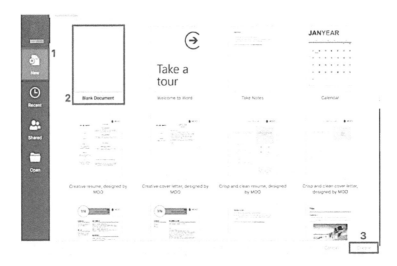

Note: Apart from clicking on Blank Document, You can create a new document or template by using the following methods or techniques right from the front view of the File tab.

- Searching online for a template
- Choosing a template
- Choosing a personal template

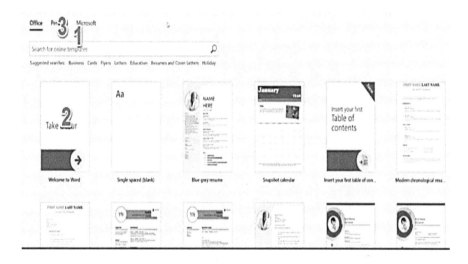

Displaying your Documents In Different Ways

There are different ways to display your documents to see. However, there are two techniques to use to change the views of your documents, and they are as follow:

- **Using the Status bar**: Go to the **Status bar** and click on any of the three View buttons on the right-hand side; **Read Mode, Print Layout, and Web Layout.**

- **The View Tab**: Go to the **View tab**, and click on any of the five buttons in the **View group**. In addition to the View group, is **Outline and Draft Views**

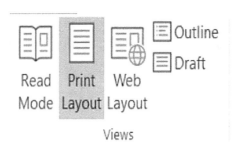

Views

- **Read Mode:** This view is also referred to as Full-Screen Reading. This allows you to maximize the Word window on the screen, in such a way that all the toolbars are removed for easy reading of the documents.
- **Print Layout:** This view displays the document the way it should be when printed out. This is the default view.
- **Web Layout:** This displays the document the way it should appear on the web page.
- **Outline:** This displays the document in the outline where content is displayed in a bulleted form.
- **Draft:** This view displays the document in draft mode for easy and quick editing. When the document is displayed in this mode, the headers and footers are not visible to see.

Splitting the Screen

Splitting your screen comes in handy when you want some contents in your documents to correlate with each other. Rather than moving to and fro on the same page, all you need to do is split your screen into two parts. To split your screen, follow the steps given below

- Go to the **View** tab and click on the **Split** button

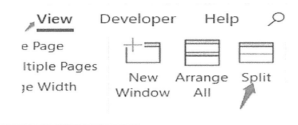

- Drag the gray line to adjust the gray line to where you want the Split to be

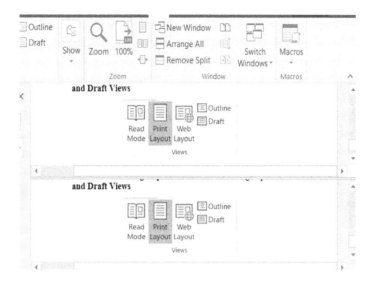

- You can choose any view of your choices to any of the split screens; you can make the first screen an outline view and the second screen to be a draft view.

Techniques Needed to Navigate Through Your Documents

At times, your documents may contain a lot of pages, and this may take a lot of time going through every page in the documents. Here, I will be showing you some techniques in Word to quickly move around your documents.

Using the Shortcut keys

There are some keys in Word that allows you quickly browse through your documents with ease, these keys are listed in the table below

Shortcut keys	Functions
PgUp	To move up the length of the screen

PgDown	To move down the length of the screen
Home	To move to the start of the line
End	To move to the end of the line
Crtl + PgUp	To move to the previous page in the document.
Crtl + PgDown	To move to the next page in the document.
Ctrl + Home	To move to the top of the document.
Ctrl + End	To move to the bottom of the documents.

Using the Navigation Pane

The Navigation Pane is another feature that allows you to move through your document with ease, especially when you have a lengthy document to go through. To display the Navigation Pane, follow the steps below

Go to the **View tab** and select the **Navigation Pane** check box

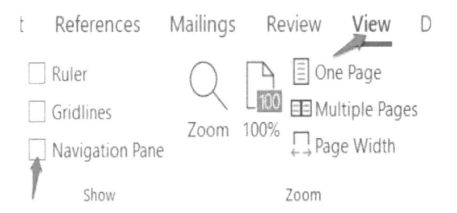

- Move to the left-hand side of the screen to select **any of the following options**

o **The Header Tab:** Here, headings in your document are displayed exactly like a table of content where you get to click on the headings to navigate through the documents.

o **Pages Tab:** This displays the thumbnails of every page in the document. To move from one page to the other, click on the page thumbnails. To know the exact page you are viewing, all the thumbnails are numbered with their page numbers.

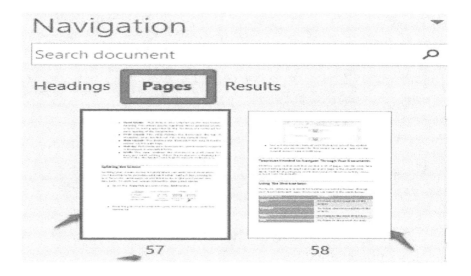

Using the Go to Command

Another technique to quickly move around your document is to use the Go To command. To use the Go To command, follow the steps given below

- Go to the **Home tab,** locate the **Find button** at the upper right-hand side of the screen, and then click on **Go To**

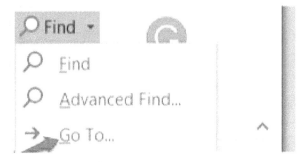

- Here on this page, the **Find and Replace** dialog box is displayed. Move **to Go to what menu** to select any of the listed options to navigate through your documents.

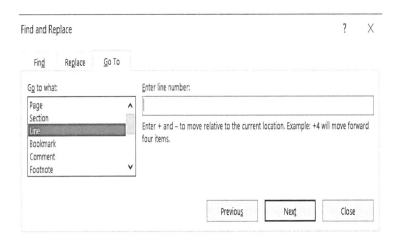

- You can also use the **Previous** or **Next** button to move around the documents.

Injecting a File into a Document

One of the most interesting facts about using Word 365 is that you can insert a file into your document, without having to type all over again or use the copy and paste method. To insert a file into your document, follow the steps below

- Move the mouse cursor to where you wish to add the document.
- Go to the **Insert tab,** click on **Object** in the **Text** group

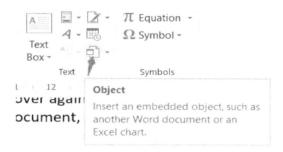

- Click on **Text from File in the Object** drop-down list

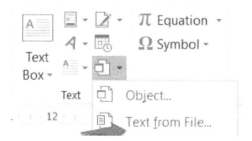

- In the **Insert File** dialog box, select the file to be inserted, and then click on the **Insert button.**

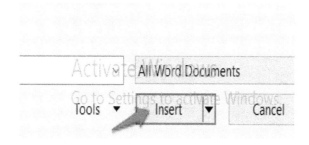

NOTE: You can insert more than one file with the Text from File command. All you need to do is select the files in the Insert File dialog box and then click on Insert.

Using the Undo and Repeat Command

The Undo Command

One of the most important commands you should not joke with is the Undo command. The Undo command helps to revert to the last change you made to your document. This comes in handy when you mistakenly add some unwanted details to your document.

The Undo button is located on the Quick Access toolbar, and you can click on the Undo button drop-down list to view the previous actions executed in your document.

To undo your most recent changes, click on the **Undo** button on the **Quick Access** toolbar or use the shortcut keys **Ctrl + Z**

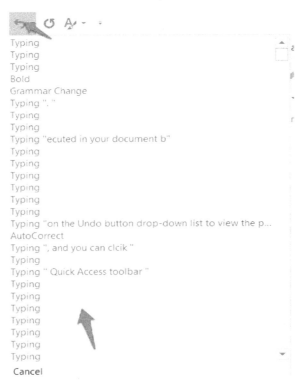

The Repeat Command

The Repeat command is the opposite of the Undo command. The Repeat command repeats the last action executed in your document. To repeat the last action, click on the **Repeat** button in the **Quick Access** toolbar or use the shortcut keys **Ctrl + Y**

Using the Zoom Controls

With the Zoom controls, you can adjust the size of your computer screen. To use the Zoom controls, use any of the following techniques

- **Zoom button**: Go to the **Status bar** at the right-hand side of the screen on the **Zoom Slider** to zoom in or out

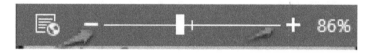

- **Zoom Slider**: Drag the **Zoom** slider shrink or enlarge the screen in the Status bar.

- **Zoom Dialog Box**: Go to the **View** tab and click on **Zoom** in the Zoom group. The **Zoom** dialog box is displayed where you can zoom in or zoom out.

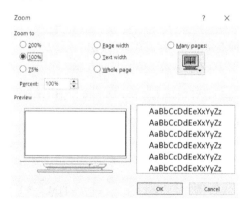

Using Word 365 to Read Your Document

Instead of reading the content of a Text in a document yourself, Word 365 can do that for you. To get Word 365 to read your text for you, follow the steps given below

- Open the document you want to read out

- Ensure that your document view is in **Print Layout** or **Web Layout** view.

- Place the insertion point to where you want to start the reading from

- Go to the **Review** tab and click on the **Read Aloud** button

- To stop word from reading, click on the **Read Aloud** button again

Saving a File

It is not enough that you create a new file, you must ensure to save it. Failure to save your file will only cause you to lose your file, especially where there is a power outage or malfunction with the computer system. It is very important to always save your file every ten minutes.

To save a file, use any of the following techniques

- Go to the **File** tab and click on the **Save** menu

- Click the **Save** button located in the **Quick Access** toolbar

- Press **Ctrl + S**

Saving a File for the First Time

Saving a file for the first time, the Save As window appears where you enter the name of the file and the location where you want the file to be saved.

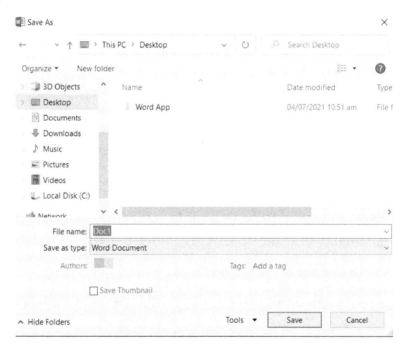

Saving Auto Recovery Information

The Auto Recovery command is a feature in Word 365 that automatically saves the document you are working on at specific intervals. With the Auto Recovery command, data lost due to computer or power failure can be recovered

To enable the Auto Recovery command, follow the steps given below

- Go to the **File** tab and click on **Options**

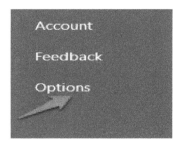

- In the **Options** dialog box, select the **Save** category

- Enter the minute interval in the **Save AutoRecover Information Every** box

- Then click on **Ok**

Opening Files

To open a file, follow the steps provided below

- Go to the File tab and click on Open

- Select the name of the file you wish to open on the **Recent** list

- In case the file is not on the **Recent** list, click on the location (**This PC, OneDrive,** etc.) to locate the file.

- Select the file and then click on the **Open** button.

Closing a File

To close a file, use any of the following techniques

- Go to the **File** tab and click on **Close**

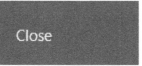

Close

- Click on the Close button at the upper right corner of the window.

- Press **Alt + F4**

MANIPULATING TEXTS CHAPTER FOUR

This chapter is focused on how words texts are used to get the desired results while working on Word 365. Here in this chapter, you will learn some techniques on how to delete, copy, move, change text fonts, change texts, and lots more.

Moving and Copying Text

One of the basic things done with texts in your documents is to copy or move. To copy or move texts in your documents, use any of the following methods.

- **Drag and drop**: To move text, use the mouse to highlight or select the text, and drag it to the desired location. To copy the text, select or highlight the text, hold down the Ctrl key, and then drag the text.
- **Using the Clipboard:** Another way to move or copy text is to use the Clipboard. To locate the Clipboard, go to the **Home tab**, and click on the **Clipboard** on the left-hand side.

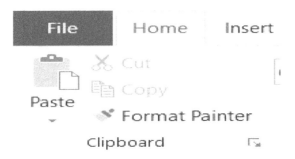

To move or copy text, select the text and click on **Cut** or **Copy** on the **Clipboard**. Go to where you want the texts to be moved or copied to, then click on **Paste** on the **Clipboard** group. Here the texts will be moved or copied to the desired location.

Deleting Texts

While typing words on your document, there are times you will need to delete some texts and replace them with other texts. To delete texts in your documents, use any of the following techniques

- Select the texts and press the **Backspace key** or **Delete key**
- Select the text and start typing the new texts. Doing this automatically removes the old texts and replaces them with the new texts.

Adjusting the Text Alignments

One of the most important parts of Word is text alignment. Text alignment controls how your texts are positioned or placed with the page margin.

The text alignments are categorized into four

- Left Alignment
- Center
- Right Alignment
- Justify

To locate the text alignments, click on the **Home tab**, go to the **Paragraph** group, and select any alignment of your choice.

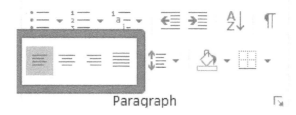

Paragraph

- **Left Alignment:** This aligns the content in your document with the left margin. You can also use the shortcut keys Ctrl + L to align your document to the left margin.

Start by making sure that Office knows which language you want to speak. On the Home tab, click the down-arrow on the Dictate button and select a language or regional language from the drop-down list.
Place the cursor where you want the words to appear and follow these steps to dictate to Word, PowerPoint, or Outlook:

- **Center:** This aligns the content in your document to the center of the page. You can also use the shortcut keys Ctrl + E to align your document to the center of the page.

Start by making sure that Office knows which language you want to speak. On the Home tab, click the down-arrow on the Dictate button and select a language or regional language from the drop-down list.
Place the cursor where you want the words to appear and follow these steps to dictate to Word, PowerPoint, or Outlook:

- **Right Alignment:** ` This aligns the content of your document with the right margin. You can also use the shortcut keys Ctrl + R to align your document to the left margin

Start by making sure that Office knows which language you want to speak. On the Home tab, click the down-arrow on the Dictate button and select a language or regional language from the drop-down list.
Place the cursor where you want the words to appear and follow these steps to dictate to Word, PowerPoint, or Outlook:

- **Justify:** This aligns the content of your document evenly between the margin. You can also use the shortcut keys Ctrl + J to justify the content of your document.

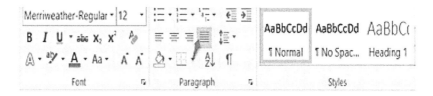

Start by making sure that Office knows which language you want to speak. On the Home tab, click the down-arrow on the Dictate button and select a language or regional language from the drop-down list.
Place the cursor where you want the words to appear and follow these steps to dictate to Word, PowerPoint, or Outlook:

Modifying the Look of Your Text

You can decide to change the way your text looks by adjusting the font, font, style, font sizes, etc. let's quickly go into how to perform these operations

Changing the Fonts in Your Text

The font in your texts can be changed into Times New Roman, Calibri Light, Calibri, Agency FB, Arial, Arial Black, Arial Narrow, etc.

To change the font of your text, do the following

- Go to the **Home tab** and go to the **Font group**

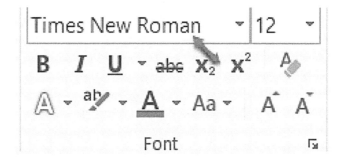

- Click on the **Font button** to apply the font to the text

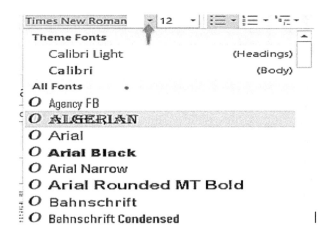

Changing the Font Sizes in Your Text

To change the font size of your text, do the following

- Go to the **Home tab** and go to the **Font group**

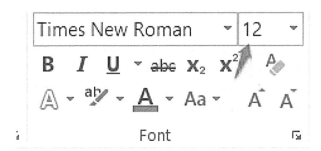

- Click on the **Font size button** to apply the font size to the text

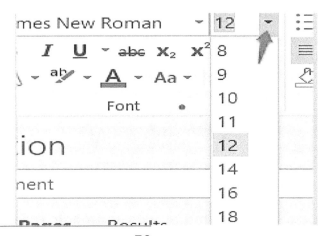

Changing the Font Syles in Your Text

Word has four major font styles you can use and they are as follow

- **Regular**: This implies that no font syle is applied to your texts
- **Bold**: This helps to bolden your text.
- **Italic**: This helps to italicize your texts.
- **Underline**: This helps to underline your texts

To apply any of the font syles

- Go to the **Home tab** and move to the **Font group**
- Then select any of the **Font** Styles as shown in the image below

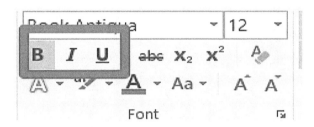

Word 365	Regular
Word 365	Bold
Word 365	Italics
Word 365	underline

NOTE: You can use shortcut keys Ctrl + B, Ctrl + I, and Ctrl + U for Bold, Italics, and Underline respectively.

Changing the Font Color of Your Text

Word 365 allows you to change the font color of your document. To do this, follow the steps below

- Select the text you wish to change its font color
- From the **Home tab**, go to the Font group and click on the **Font Color button**

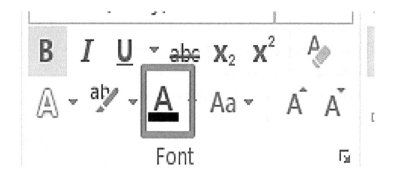

- Click on the color you want to effect the change

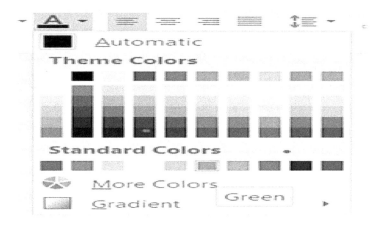

Applying Text Effects to Your Text

You can change the way your text looks by changing its fill, outline, or even adding effects such as shadows, reflections, glow, etc. to it.

To apply the text effect to your text, follow the steps below

- Select the text you wish to apply the effect to
- From the **Home tab**, go to the Font group and click on the **Text Effect button**

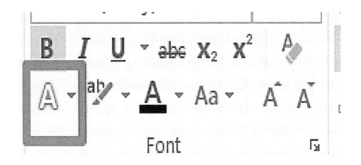

- Click on the effect you want

Applying Case to Your Text

Change case in command in word, under the font group, that changes lowercase letters to uppercase and vice versa. The change case is categorized into 5 places; sentence case, lowercase, uppercase, capitalize each word, and toggle case.

Sentence Case

This command capitalizes the first letter in the first word in each paragraph, while the other words are written in lowercase except for words that carry proper names.

To change your text to sentence case, follow the steps below

- Select the text you wish to apply the effect to
- From the **Home tab**, go to the Font group and click on the **Change Case button**
- Select **Sentence Case** to apply the case to the texts.

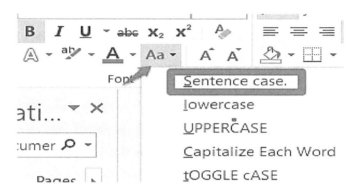

- The image below shows the texts changed to sentence case

Change Case in a command in Word, under the Font group , that chsnges lowercase letters to uppercase and vice versa. The Change Case is categorized in 5 places; Sentenec case, lowercase, Uppercase, Capitalize each word, and Toggle case.

Lowercase

This command changes all the texts in the paragraph to small letters unless they are proper names.

To change your text to lowercase, follow the steps below

- Select the text you wish to apply the effect to
- From the **Home tab**, go to the Font group and click on the **Change Case button**
- Select **Lowercase** to apply the case to the texts.

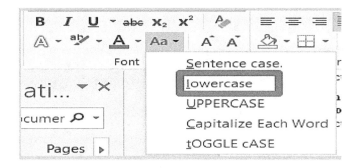

- The image below shows the texts changed to lowercase

change case in a command in word, under the font group , that chsnges lowercase letters to uppercase and vice versa. the change case is categorized in 5 places; sentenec case, lowercase, uppercase, capitalize each word, and toggle case.

Uppercase

This command changes all the letters in each paragraph to be in capital letters. To change the letters to uppercase, follow the steps below

- Select the text you wish to apply the effect to
- From the **Home tab**, go to the Font group and click on the **Change Case button**
- Select **Uppercase t**o apply the case to the texts.

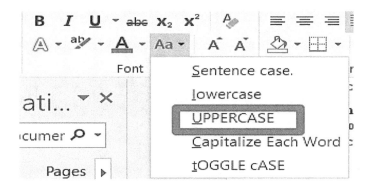

- The image below shows the texts changed to uppercase

CHANGE CASE IN A COMMAND IN WORD, UNDER THE FONT GROUP , THAT CHSNGES LOWERCASE LETTERS TO UPPERCASE AND VICE VERSA. THE CHANGE CASE IS CATEGORIZED IN 5 PLACES; SENTENEC CASE, LOWERCASE, UPPERCASE, CAPITALIZE EACH WORD, AND TOGGLE CASE.

Capitalize Each Word

This command capitalizes the first letter of each word in every paragraph in the document.

To capitalize each letter in your words, follow the steps below

- Select the text you wish to apply the effect to
- From the **Home tab**, go to the Font group and click on the **Change Case button**
- Select **Capitalize Each Word** to apply the case to the texts.

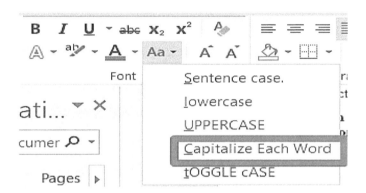

- The image below shows the texts changed to uppercase

Change Case In A Command In Word, Under The Font Group , That Chsnges Lowercase Letters To Uppercase And Vice Versa. The Change Case Is Categorized In 5 Places; Sentenec Case, Lowercase, Uppercase, Capitalize Each Word, And Toggle Case.

Toggle Case

This is the opposite of Capitalize Each Word. This command changes the first letter of each word to lowercase.

To toggle each letter in your words, follow the steps below

- Select the text you wish to apply the effect to
- From the **Home tab**, go to the Font group and click on the **Change Case button**
- Select **tOGGLE cASE t**o apply the case to the texts.

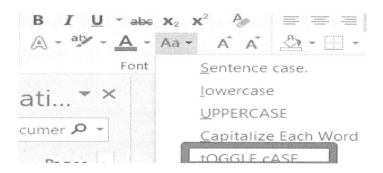

- The image below shows the texts changed to toggle case

cHANGE cASE iN a cOMMAND iN wORD, uNDER tHE fONT gROUP, tHAT cHSNGES lOWERCASE lETTERS tO uPPERCASE aND vICE vERSA. tHE cHANGE cASE iS cATEGORIZED iN 5 pLACES; sENTENEC cASE, lOWERCASE, uPPERCASE, cAPITALIZE eACH wORD, aND tOGGLE cASE.

Inserting Symbols into your document

Not every symbol can be found on your keyboard and this can be annoying at times. However, do not panic, you can also get any symbol you need. To locate any symbol on Word, follow the steps given below

- From the **Insert tab**, go to **Symbol group** and then click on **Symbol**

Symbols

- Here on this page, the **Symbol** dialog box is displayed, where you can choose any symbol of your choice.

- To get a wide range of symbols, click on **More Symbols**

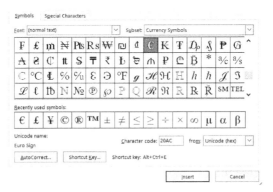

Speaking Words Rather Than Typing

One of the new features in Word 365 is the Dictate tool. The Dictate tool allows you to speak the words you will have displayed on the screen, rather than using the keyboard. Provided the microphone in your computer works perfectly well and you can say the words clear and slow, the computer will have the words displayed on the screen,

To use the Dictate tool, follow the steps given below

- Go to the **Home** tab and click on the **Dictate** button at the right-hand side of the menu bar
- Once the red circle appears on the **Dictate** button
- Start talking slowly and clearly and when you are done, click the **Dictate** button.

CHAPTER FIVE

LAYING OUT TEXT AND PAGES

This chapter is focused mainly on how to format text and pages. Going through this chapter, you will learn how to formatting skills such as inserting a section break in your document, breaking a line, starting a new page, setting up and changing the margins, indenting paragraphs and first lines, numbering pages, and lots more.

Inserting Section Break in Your Document

Section breaks are used to divide documents into different chapters and add formatting such as headers and footers, columns, page borders, margins, page numbering, etc. to each section.

To insert a section break in your document, follow the steps below

- Click on where you want to insert the section break
- Go to the **Layout** tab and click on the **Breaks** button

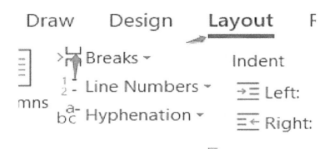

- In the Break drop-down list, select any of the following options
  - Next **Page**: This inserts a section break and starts the new section break on the next page.
  - **Continuous:** This inserts a section break and starts the new section break on the same page.
  - **Even Page**: This inserts a section break and starts the new session on the next even-numbered page.

- **Odd Page**: This inserts a section break and starts the new section on the next odd-numbered page.

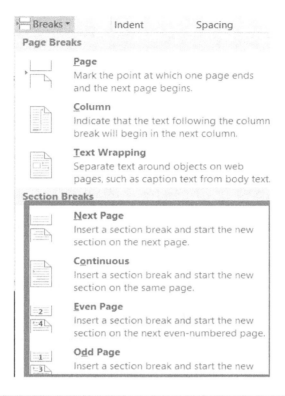

Deleting a Section Break

To delete the section break inserted into your document, change the view of your document to Draft view so that you can see where the section line is inserted. Click on the dotted line, and then press the Delete key.

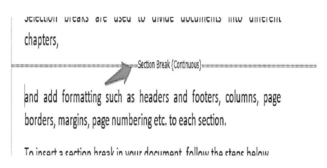

Inserting Page Break

Page break separates the content between pages. When the page break is inserted, the text starts at the beginning of the page.

To insert a page break in your document, follow the steps below

- Click on where you want to insert the section break
- Go to the **Layout** tab and click on the **Breaks** button

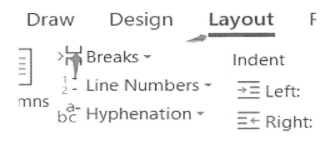

- In the Break drop-down list, select any of the following options
  - Page: This marks the point at which one page ends and the next page begins.
  - Column: This specifies the text following the column break that will begin in the next column.
  - Text Wrapping: This separates text around objects on web pages, such as caption from text from the body text.

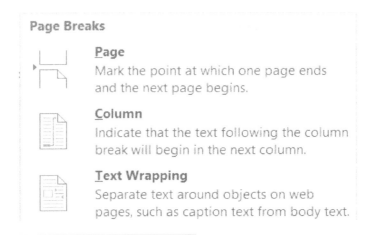

Deleting Page Break

To delete the page break inserted into your document, the first thing you need to do is ensure that the page break dotted line is visible in the document. If it is not, go to the **Home** tab, in the **Paragraph** group, and click on **Show or Hide**

Change the view of your document to Draft view so that you can see where the section line is inserted. Click on the dotted line, and then press the Delete

dictate·to·Word,·PowerPoint,·or·Outlook:¶

Breaking a Line

You can break the line of a text before reaching the right margin without starting a new paragraph. All you need to do is press Shift + Enter. See the image below to see the result of the shortcut keys

Start by making sure that Office knows which language you want to speak. On the Home tab, click the xdown-arrow on the Dictate button and select a language or regional language from the drop-down list. Place the cursor where you want the words to appear and follow these steps to dictate to Word, PowerPoint, or Outlook:

Starting a New Page

When you begin to type documents on Word, you move to the next page when the current page is filled up.

To start or open a new page, follow the steps given below

- Go to the Insert Tab and click on any of the following
    - Blank Page: This allows you to open a new page by adding a blank page anywhere in your document.
    - **Page Break:** This also allows you to open a new page by ending the current page to open another one

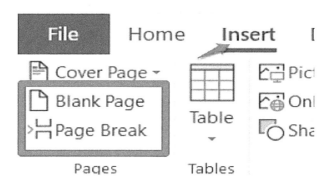

Setting Up and Adjusting the Page Margins

Margins are the blank spaces between the text and edges of your document. Margins are essential in your documents because they make your documents look presentable and professional. The default margin of the document is Normal. However, you can change your margins to any type that suits your documents. There are three different ways to adjust the page margins of your documents:

- Adjusting page margin using the ruler.
- Adjusting page margin using preset margins.
- Adjusting page margin by using custom margins.

Adjusting Page Margin Using Ruler

You can adjust the margins in your document by using the ruler, to do this, follow the steps provided below

- Go to the **View tab** and click on **Ruler** in the **Show Group**

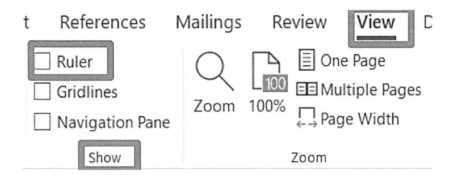

- Hover your cursor over the inner border of the gray area on the left or right end of the horizontal ruler until your cursor becomes a double arrow. Then move the double-arrow cursor to the left or right to adjust the margin.

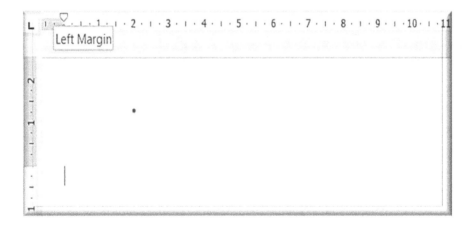

- Hover your cursor over the inner border of the gray area of the top or bottom of the vertical ruler until your cursor becomes a double arrow. Then move the double-arrow cursor up or down to adjust the margin.

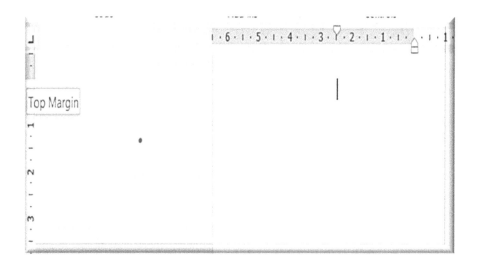

NOTE: This method of adjusting the page margin is best used for short documents. In case the documents are too long, use the preset or custom margin methods.

Adjusting Page Margin Using Preset Margins

To adjust the page margin of your documents, follow the steps given below

- Go to the **Layout** tab and select **Margins**
- Select any of the options in the Margins drop-down menu
  - Normal
  - Narrow
  - Moderate
  - Wide
  - Mirrored (This is for binding documents like a book.)
  - Office 2003 Default
  - Custom margin

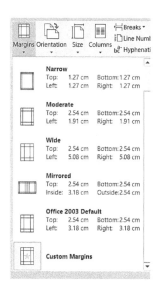

NOTE: The preset margins only take effect on your current section.

Adjusting Page Margin by Using Custom Margins

To adjust the margin using the custom margins, do the following

- Go to the **Page Layout** tab.
- Click on the **dialog box launcher** in **the Page Setup** group.

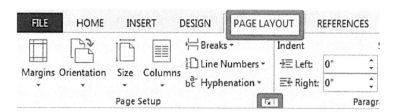

- On the Page Setup dialog box, do the following
  - Input the new margins in inches in the Top, Left, Bottom, and Right text boxes
  - Enter the figure in the **Gutter box**, and also enter the position in the **Gutter position box**
  - Change the page orientation to either **Portrait** or **Landscape**

- o Set the Multiple pages to either **Normal, Mirror margins, Two pages per sheet,** or **Book fold.**
- o Select a location in the **Apply to the** menu such as **This section, The point forward, Whole document.**
- Click the **Ok** button to close the dialog box.

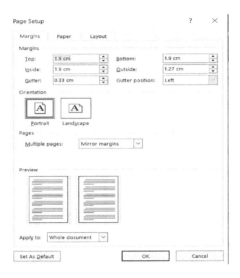

Indenting Your Paragraph

Indentation in Word is the increase or decrease of space between the left and right margin of a paragraph. There are three ways to indent a paragraph in Word:

- Indent single paragraphs with the tab key
- Indent all paragraphs with the ruler
- Indent all paragraphs with the Paragraph dialog box

Indent Single Paragraphs with the Tab key

The fastest and easiest method to insert an indent single paragraph is to use the Tab key. To use the Tab key to insert indent, follow the step below

- Insert your cursor at the start of the paragraph
- Press the **Tab key** on the keyboard

Indentation in Word is the increase or decrease of space between the left and right of a paragraph. There are three ways you to indent paragraph in Word:

Indent All Paragraphs with the Ruler

You can indent all paragraphs in your document using the ruler. Follow the steps given below to indent all paragraphs using the rule:

- Insert the cursor into a paragraph
- Go to the **Home tab** and click on **Select** under the **Editing group**

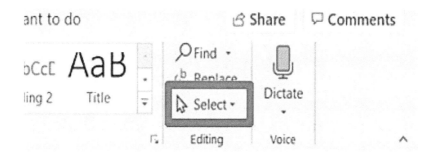

- In the drop-down menu, click on **Select Text with Similar Formatting**

- Go to the **View tab** and click on **Ruler** in the **Show Group**

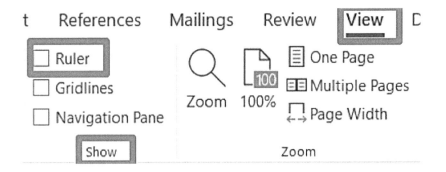

- Move the top ruler marker at the right to the indent length you want. As you move the ruler marker, the paragraph is indented

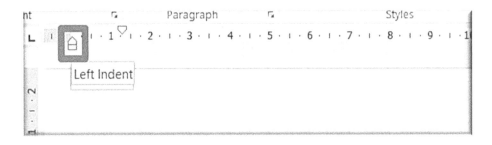

Indent All paragraphs with the Paragraph Dialog Box

To indent all paragraphs using the Paragraph dialog box, follow the steps below:

- Insert the cursor into a paragraph
- Go to the **Home tab** and click on **Select** under the **Editing group**

- In the drop-down menu, click on **Select Text with Similar Formatting**

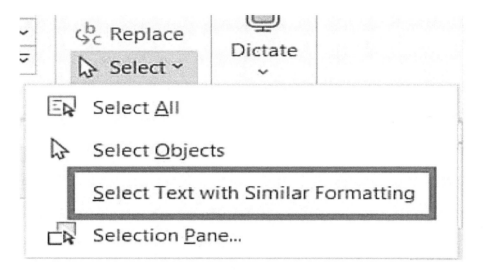

- Click on **Paragraph group's dialog box launcher** to display the **Paragraph dialog box**

- **In the Paragraph dialog box, set the following options:**
  - Select the **Special** menu arrow and click on **the First line** in the Special drop-down menu
  - Adjust the length of the indent by using the increment arrows.
  - You can also make additional adjustments to the Alignment or Spacing menu

- Click on the **Ok** button to save the changes made and close the Paragraph dialog box.

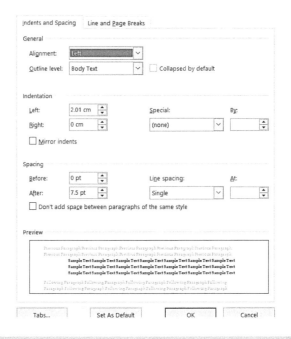

The Tab Selector

The tab selector is found above the vertical ruler on the left. To see the name of the tab selector, hover the mouse over the tab selector.

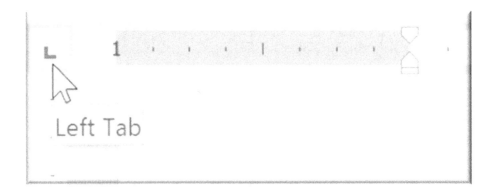

The following are the types of tab stops

- **Left Tab**: This left-aligns the text at the tab stop.

- **Center Tab**: This centers the text around the tab stop.
- **Right Tab**: This right-aligns the text at the tab stop
- **Decimal Tab**: This aligns decimal numbers using the decimal point.
- **Bar Tab**: This draws a vertical line on the document.
- **First Line Indent:** This helps to insert the indent marker on the ruler and indent the first line of text in a paragraph
- **Hanging Indent:** This inserts the hanging indent marker and indents all lines other than the first line.

Working with Page Numbers

Numbering the pages in your document is very important, especially when working with a document with so many pages. Page numbering comes in a wide range of number formats and they can be modified to meet your needs and specifications. You can insert your page numbers in the header, footer, or side margin.

Adding Page Numbers to Your Documents

To add a page number to your document, follow the steps giving below:

- Go to the **Insert** tab and click on **Page Number** under **Header & Footer** group

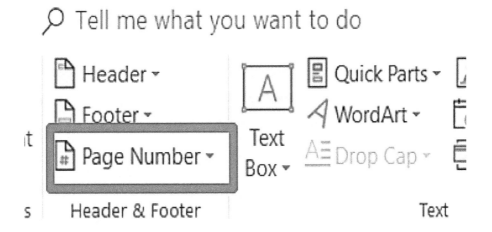

- On the drop-down list, select either **Top of Page**, **Bottom of Page**, **Page Margins,** or **Current Position.**

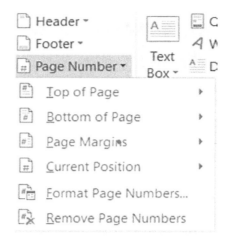

- Then select any of the styles of header you desire and the page numbering will appear on the page

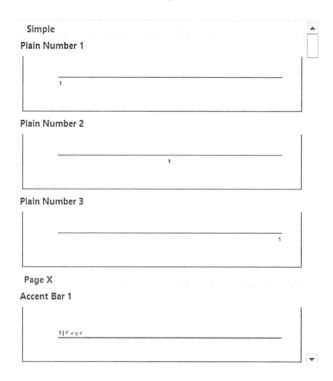

Adding Page Number to Header or Footer

In case you have a header or footer in your document, and you wish to add a page number to it, follow the steps

- Double click on the **Header** or **Footer**

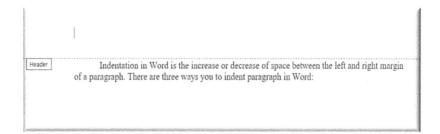

- On the **Design tab**, click on **Page Number** and click on **Current Position. Then click on the page numbering style you want**

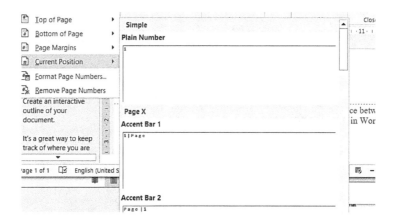

Changing the Page Number Format

To change the page number format, follow the steps below

- Go to the **Insert tab** and click on **Page Number** under **Header & Footer** group

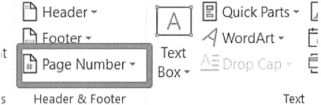

- Click on Page Number Format

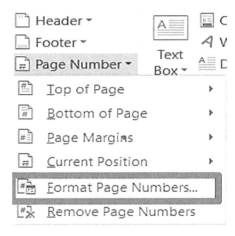

- In the **Page Number Format** dialog box, choose any format in the **Number Format** drop-down list.

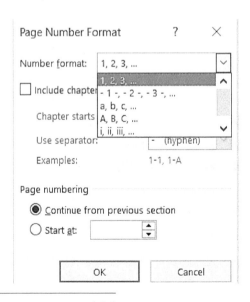

Hiding Page Number on the First Page

You may not want your documents to show the page number of the first page. And to get this done, follow the steps below

- Double click on the **Header** or **Footer**

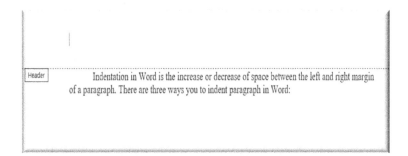

- Go to the **Design** tab, click on **Different First Page,** and the header and footer will disappear from the first page

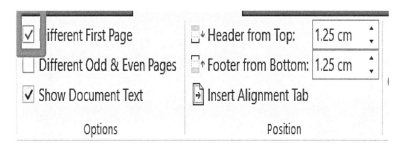

Working with Header and Footer

The header is a section of the document that is displayed at the top margin to give a short description to the reader, while the footer is also another section of the document that is displayed at the bottom margin to give a short description to the reader. The header and footer contain information such as page number, dates, and even the author's name.

Take note of the following while working with the header and footer

- To edit, read, enter, or delete your header or footer, you will need to switch to Print Layout view.
- To use the header and footer tools, you will need to display the Design tab by double-clicking on the header or footer.
- To place different headers and footers in the same document, you will need to create a new section.
- To close the header footer, click on the Close Header and Footer button or double-click outside the header or footer.

Inserting a Header or Footer in Your Document

To insert a header or footer in your document, follow the steps below

- Go to the **Insert tab** and click on **Header** or **Footer**

- Select the style you wish to use

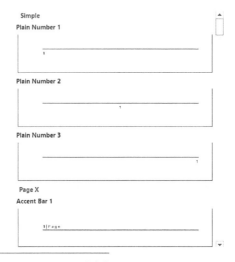

- Enter the desired information into the header or footer

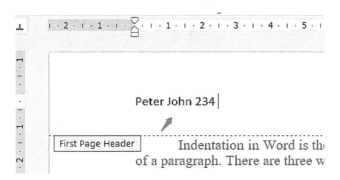

- When you are done, click on **Close Header and Footer** or press the **Esc** key.

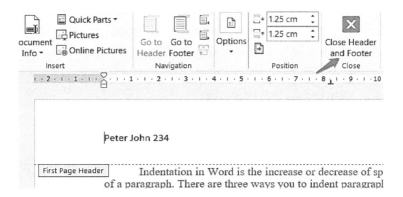

- Finally, the header or footer will appear on your document

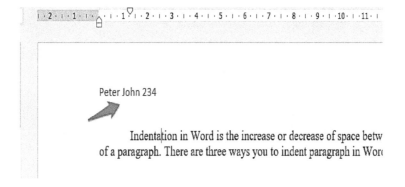

Editing Header or Footer in Your Document

To edit the header or footer, double-click on the header or footer. The cursor appears on the footer or header where you edit the text.

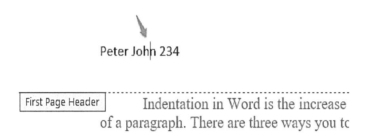

Note: You can also edit your header or footer by going to **Header** or **Footer,** and then select **Edit Header** or **Edit Footer**

Removing the Header or Footer in Your Document

You can remove your header or footer by going to **Header** or **Footer,** and then select **Remove Header** or **Remove Footer**

Adding Date and Time to Your Header or Footer

At times, you may want to add a date and time to your header or footer, just to show when it was created. To add the date and time to your header and footer, follow the steps given below

- Double click anywhere on the **Header** or **Footer**
- In the **Design** tab, click on **the Date and Time** command

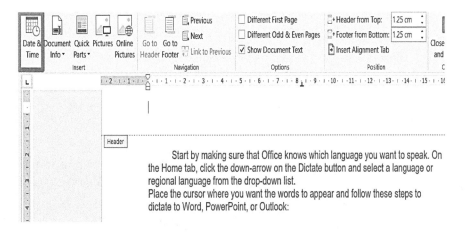

- In the **Date and Time** dialog box, choose the date or time format you want and click on **Update Automatically**, if you want the date and time to update each time you open the document.

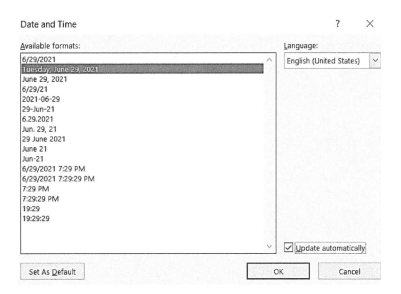

- Here, the date appears on the header or footer.

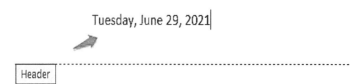

Tuesday, June 29, 2021

Header

Start by making sure that Office kno
the Home tab, click the down-arrow on the
regional language from the drop-down list.
Place the cursor where you want the words
dictate to Word, PowerPoint, or Outlook:

Adjusting Line Spacing

Line spacing can be referred to as the space between each line in a
paragraph. You can format your line spacing to be one-line spacing,
double line spacing, or any other spacing available. The default spacing
in Word is 1.08 lines, which is a little bit larger than a one-line spacing.

To adjust the line spacing in your document, follow the steps given below

- Select the text you wish to adjust
- Go to the **Home tab** and click on **Line and Paragraph Spacing command**
- Then select the desired spacing options from the drop-down menu

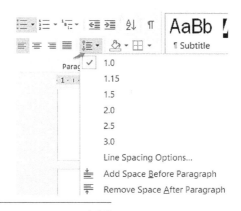

- There are additional spacing options in the Paragraph dialog box. To view the paragraph dialog box, go to the **Home tab** and click on the **Paragraph** group button.

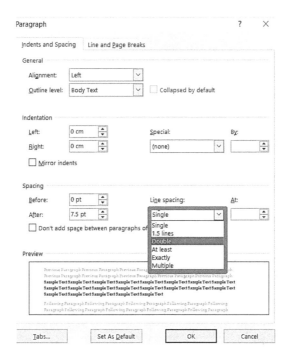

The following are the additional options for line spacing

- **At least**: This option allows you to set minimum point size to use for line spacing.
- **Exactly**: This allows you to set the exact point size to use between the lines of the selected paragraphs.
- **Multiples**: This allows you to put in a precise multiple to use for spacing.

Adjusting Paragraph Spacing

Paragraph spacing is the space between paragraphs in a document. Paragraph spacing allows you to separates the headings and the subheadings.

- Select the paragraphs or paragraphs you wish to adjust

- Go to the **Home** tab, click on **Line and Paragraph Spacing command** and select **Add Space Before Paragraph** or **Remove Space Before Paragraph**

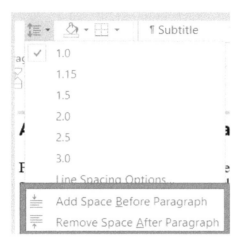

- In the drop-down option above, you can select **Line Spacing Options** to open the Paragraph dialog option. Here you get to control the level of space that is before and after the paragraphs in the documents.

Numbered and Bulleted Lists

A numbered list is used when the information in your document must be in a specific order, while a bulleted list is any symbol used to highlight items in a list.

Creating a Numbered List

To create a numbered list, follow the steps given below

- Select the text you wish to list
- Go to the **Home tab** and click on **Numbering** under the **Paragraph group.** Click on the styles of numbering you want.

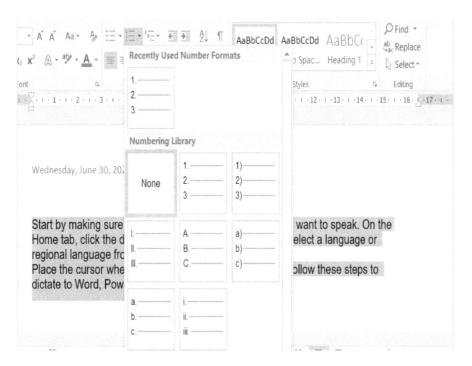

- Here on this page, the texts are numbered

1. Start by making sure that Office knows which language you want to speak. On the Home tab, click the down-arrow on the Dictate button and select a language or
2. regional language from the drop-down list.
3. Place the cursor where you want the words to appear and follow these steps to
4. dictate to Word, PowerPoint, or Outlook:

Creating a Bulleted List

To create a bulleted list, follow the steps given below

- Select the text you wish to list

- Go to the **Home tab** and click on **Bullet** under the **Paragraph group.** Click on the styles of bullet you want.

- Here on this page, the texts are bulleted

- Start by making sure that Office knows which language you want to speak. On the Home tab, click the down-arrow on the Dictate button and select a language or
- regional language from the drop-down list.
- Place the cursor where you want the words to appear and follow these steps to
- dictate to Word, PowerPoint, or Outlook:

Creating Your Own Numbered List

You can create your own numbered list without using the numbering in the Numbered List Library. To do this, follow the steps below:

- Go to the **Home tab** and click on **Numbering** under the **Paragraph group.**
- In the drop-down menu, click on **Define New Number Format**

- In the **Define Number Format dialog box,** set the following:

  - Number style
  - Number Format
  - Alignment

- Then click on **Ok**

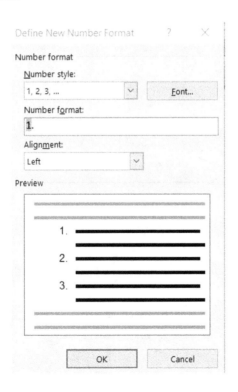

Creating Your Own Bulleted List

You can create your own bulleted list without using the bullets in the Bulleted List Library. To do this, follow the steps below:

- Go to the **Home tab** and click on **Bullet** under the **Paragraph group.**
- In the drop-down menu, click on **Define New Bullet**

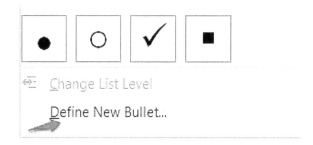

- In the **Define New Bullet dialog box**, set the following

  o Build character
  o Alignment

- Then click on **Ok**

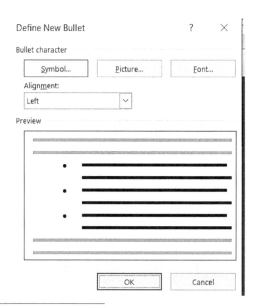

Useful Tips When Using the Number and Bullets List

When working with the list, you can use the following tips

- To end a list, press the Enter key twice after typing the last entry in the list
- To remove numbers or bullets from your text, select the list and click on the Numbering or Bullet button.
- You can adjust the indentation of the list by right-clicking anywhere in the list. Select the Adjust List Indents, and input the new measurement in the Text Indent box.
- To start a new list, right-click on the number Word inputted and select Restart at 1 on the shortcut menu.

Manage a Multilevel List

A multilevel list is a combination of numbered lists and bulleted lists.

To create a multilevel list, follow the steps provided below

- Select the list you wish to apply the multilevel list to

- Go to the **Home** tab and click on the **Multilevel** List button to select any of the different styles in the drop-down menu.

117

- Click on **Ok** and the multilevel level will be applied to the list.

Hyphenating Text

Hyphenating your text is a process of using hyphens to words at the start of a line to allow the hyphenated part to fit in at the end of the previous line.

Hyphenating Your Text Automatically

You can hyphenate your documents automatically, follow the steps given below:

- From the **Layout** tab, click on **Hyphenation** under the **Page Setup** group and select **Automatic**.

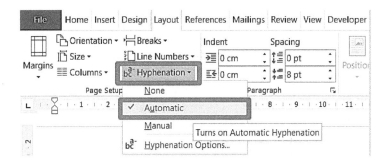

- To set how Word automatically hyphenates your document, click on **Hyphenation Options** to display the **Hyphenation** dialog box
- Set the following options in the **Hyphenation** dialog box
  - **Automatically hyphenate document:** This checkbox allows you to automatically hyphenate documents.
  - **Hyphenate words in CAPS**: This checkbox allows you to either select or deselect hyphenate words in CAPS.
  - **Hyphenation zone text box**: This allows you to indicate the amount of space to leave between the end of the last word in a line, and in the right margin.
  - **Limit consecutive hyphens to the text box:** This sets the number of consecutive lines that can be hyphenated.

- Then click on **Ok**

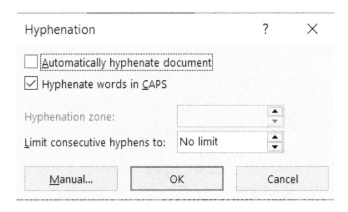

Hyphenating Your Text Manually

Hyphenating your document manually allows you to make hyphenation decisions on a case-by-case basis. To hyphenate your document manually, follow the steps given below:

- From the **Layout** tab, click on **Hyphenation** under the **Page Setup** group and select **Manual.**

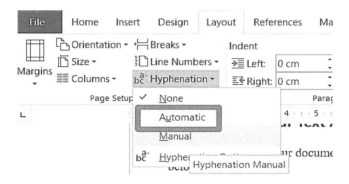

- In the **Manual Hyphenation** dialog box, set the hyphen in another location by inserting text in the Hyphenate at text box.
- Then click on **Yes**

Removing Hyphenation

To remove hyphenation from a document

- Go to the **Layout** tab, click on **Hyphenation** under the **Page Setup** group and select **None.**

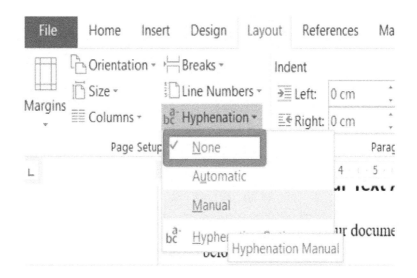

Preventing Text from Being Hyphenated

You can prevent your texts from being hyphenated, by following the steps below

- Select the text you wish not to get hyphenated
- Go to the **Home** tab and click on the **Paragraph** group button

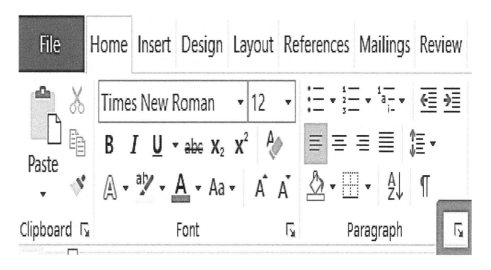

- In the **Paragraph** dialog box, select the **Line and Page Breaks** tab, and then click on the **Don't Hyphenate** check box

- Then click on **Ok**

CHAPTER SIX

EXPLORING WORD STYLES

Style is a set of formatting features such as font size, color, and alignment that can be applied to text, tables, and lists in a document, to quickly change the appearance of the document. Applying styles to your document helps to give it a professional look.

Why Should You Use Styles?

The following are the reasons why you need to use Styles while creating documents

- Styles gives your document uniform headings and subheadings
- Styles allow for efficient formatting while working with your document.
- Applying a style in your document gives you a quick way to see the headings and subheadings on the Navigation Pane.
- Applying styles to your document gives you an easy shortcut to get a table of content and a list of tables and figures automatically.

Components of Styles

The following are the components of Styles

- **Paragraph styles**: These paragraph styles control the formatting of a complete paragraph. The paragraph style has the following settings; font, paragraph, tab, border, language, bullet, numbering, and text effects. The paragraph style is denoted with the paragraph symbol (¶)
- **Character styles:** The character style can only be applied to text in a document. To apply this type of style, you will have to first select the text. The character style has the following settings font, border, language, and text effect.

- **Linked (Paragraph and character)**: These styles type can be applied to both paragraphs and text within a document. These styles can be denoted with paragraph symbol (¶) and with the letter a
- **Table styles:** These control the formatting outlook of a table in a document. The table styles have the following settings borders, shadings, alignment, and fonts.
- **List styles**: These control the formatting of the list by applying similar alignment, numbering, or bullet characters, and fonts.

Applying Styles to your Text or Paragraphs

You can apply styles to your text or paragraph by following the steps below

- Select the text or paragraph you wish to format (You can position your cursor at the beginning of the paragraph)

Style is a set of formatting features such as font size, color, and alignment that can be applied to text, tables, and lists in a document, to quickly change the appearance of the document

Applying styles to your document helps to give it a professional look.

- In the **Styles** group on the **Home** tab, click on the **More** drop-down arrow.

- Select the desired style from the drop-down menu.

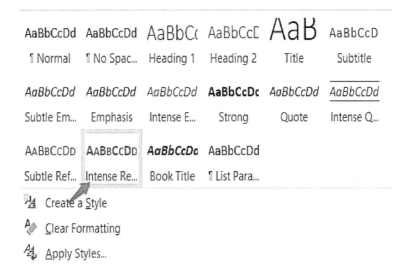

- The text selected will appear in the desired style selected.

> STYLE IS A SET OF FORMATTING FEATURES SUCH AS FONT SIZE, COLOR, AND ALIGNMENT THAT CAN BE APPLIED TO TEXT, TABLES, AND LISTS IN A DOCUMENT, TO QUICKLY CHANGE THE APPEARANCE OF THE DOCUMENT
>
> Applying styles to your document helps to give it a professional look.

Applying a Style Set

Style sets are made up of a title, heading, and paragraph styles. Style sets permit you to format all the elements in your document at once instead of modifying each of the elements separately. Before you apply the Style set, you must have assigned styles to either your paragraph, text, table or list.

Follow the procedures below to apply style set to your text or paragraph

- In the **Document Formatting** group on the **Design** tab, click on the **More** drop-down arrow.

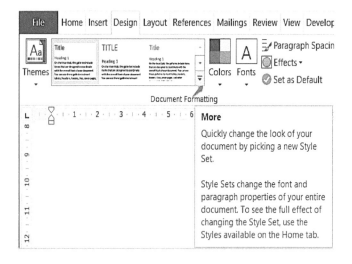

- Select the desired style from the drop-down menu.

- The style set selected will appear on the entire document.

STYLE IS A SET OF FORMATTING FEATURES SUCH AS FONT SIZE, COLOR, AND ALIGNMENT THAT CAN BE APPLIED TO TEXT, TABLES, AND LISTS IN A DOCUMENT, TO QUICKLY CHANGE THE APPEARANCE OF THE DOCUMENT

Applying styles to your document helps to give it a professional look.

Creating a New Style

There are two ways to create a new style in your document, it is either by creating it from the paragraph or the ground up. Now let's create a new style using the two methods earlier mentioned.

Creating a New Style from a Paragraph

To create a new style from a paragraph, follow the steps given below

- Select the paragraph you wish to change its formatting into a style

> Style sets is made up of title, heading, and paragraph styles. Style sets permit you to format all the elements in your document at once instead of modifying each of the elements separately. Before you apply the Style set, you must have assigned styles to either your paragraph, text, table or list.

- From the **Home** tab, open the **Styles** gallery and click on **Creating a Style**

- In the **Create New Style from the Formatting** dialog box, enter the name of the new style and then click on **Ok**

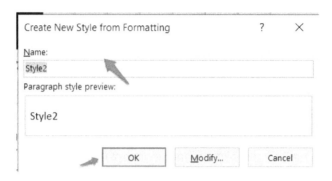

Creating a Style from the Ground up

To create a new style from the ground up, follow the steps given below

- From the **Home** tab and click on the **Styles** group button

- Here, the **Style** task pane will appear. When it appears, select the **New Style** button at the bottom of the task pane.

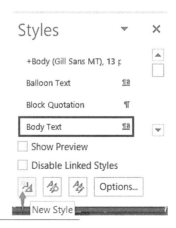

- In the **Create New Style from Formatting** dialog box, set the following options

  o **Name:** Input the description name of the new style.
  o **Style Type:** This allows you to choose any type of style (Paragraph, character, line, table, and list)
  o **Style Based On:** This allows you to choose the style to get a head start on if the new style is related to a style that is already found in the template.
  o **Style for Formatting Paragraph:** This allows you to select a style from the drop-down list if the style you are creating is related or followed by an existing style.
  o **Formatting:** This allows you to choose an option from the menu to refine your style.
  o **Add to Style Gallery:** This check box allows the style's name to appear in the Styles gallery, Style pane, and Apply Styles task pane.
  o **Automatically Update:** This updates the changes made to the styles in the document.
  o **Only in This Document/New Documents Based on This Template:** This allows you to make your style part of the template from which you created your document as well as the document itself.
  o **Format:** Clicking on this button directs you to a dialog box where you can create or refine the style.

- Then click on Ok

Modifying a Style

To modify a style, follow the steps below:

- Go to the **Home** tab, right-click on the Style you wish to change in the **Style**s group, and then click on **Modify** in the drop-down menu

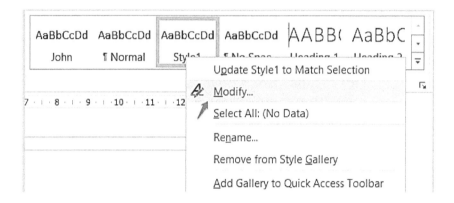

- Adjust the settings in the Modify dialog box and click on **OK**

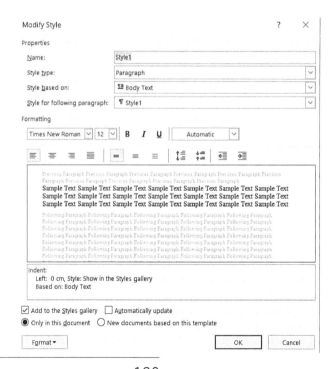

Renaming Your Styles

To change the name of your styles, follow the steps below

- Go to the **Home** tab, right-click on the Style you wish to change in the **Style**s group, and then click on **Rename** in the drop-down menu

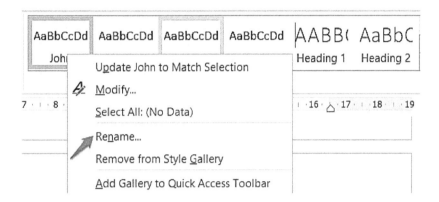

- In the **Rename Style** dialog box, enter the name and click on **Ok**

CHAPTER SEVEN

CONSTRUCTING A PERFECT TABLE IN WORD

Here in this chapter, we will be taking our time to go deeply into the table, which happens to be a major part of Word. Here in this chapter, we will be learning how to manipulate the table to suit your specifications and operations.

What is a Table

A table is a grid of cells organized into rows and columns. Tables are used to organize any form of content, be it text or numerical data for typing, editing, and formatting appropriately in your document. The following are the components of a table:

- **Cell**: This is the box that is formed when the row and column intersect.
- **Header row: This is the name of the label along** the top row that describes what is in the column.
- **Row labels**: These are the labels in the first column that explain what is in each row.
- **Borders**: These are the lines that state indicates where the rows and columns are.
- **Gridlines:** These are the gray lines that reveal where the columns and rows are. The grid lines do not appear unless they are enabled. To display the gridlines, go to (Table Tools) and click on the View Gridlines button.

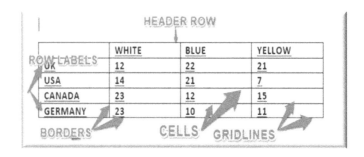

Creating a table

There are several ways to create a table in Word. Below are the method of creating a table:

- Dragging the table menu
- Inserting the table using the Insert Table dialog box
- Drawing a table
- Converting text to table
- Creating a quick table
- Constructing a table from an Excel worksheet.

Creating a Table by Dragging the Table Menu

You can create a table by dragging the table menu. To do this, follow the steps below

- Go to the **Insert** tab and click on **Table** in the **Table** group

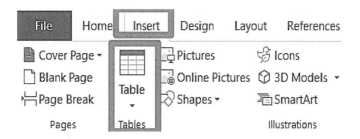

- A drop-down menu is open containing a grid. Hover over the **Grid** to select the numbers of columns and rows you want.

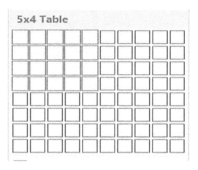

- Click on the **Grid**, release your mouse and the table will appear.

Inserting the Table Using the Insert Table Dialog Box

Another way to create a table is by using the Insert Table dialog box. To insert a table using the Insert Table dialog box, follow the steps given below:

- Go to the **Insert** tab and click on **Table** in the **Table** group

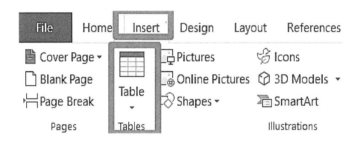

- In the drop-down menu, click on **Insert Table**

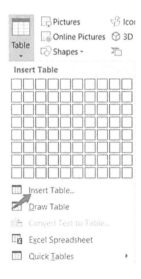

- In the Insert Table dialog box, enter the number of columns and rows and how you want the column to **Autofit.**

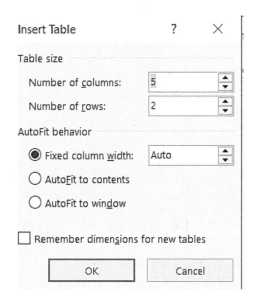

- Then click on **Ok.**

Drawing a Table

One of the many ways to create a table is by drawing. The Draw Table command allows you to design your own cells, rows, and columns border yourself. To draw a table, follow the procedures below

- Go to the **Insert** tab and click on **Table** in the **Table** group

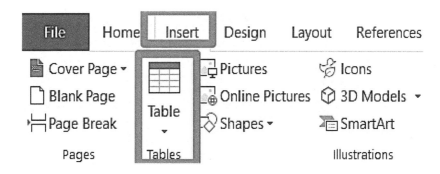

- In the drop-down menu, click on **Draw Table**

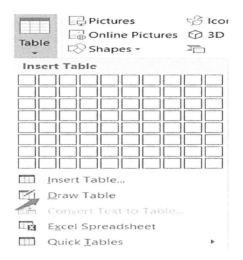

- The cursor changes to a pencil. Use the pencil to draw the rows and column

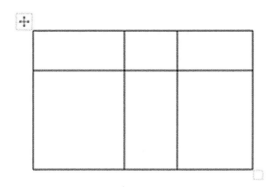

- To make any correction, use the Eraser button on the **(Table Tools) Layout tab.**

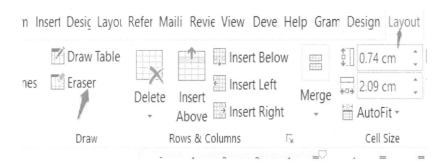

- When you are done with the drawing, click on **Esc**

Convert Text to Tables

You can create a new table by converting your texts and numbers into rows and columns. In this method of creating a new table, the number of rows is automatically determined by line breaks, and the columns are determined by the tabs, paragraph breaks, or another symbol that you have assigned manually.

To change the text to tables, follow the steps given below

- Select the texts you wish to convert to table

ORANGE, MANGO, GUAVA, ALVOCADO, GRAPE, PINEAPLE

WATER MELON, PAWPAW, CUCUMBER, CASHEW, APPLE

- Go to the **Insert** tab and click on **Table** in the **Table** group

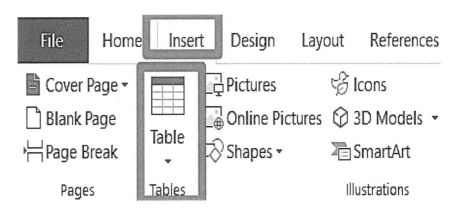

- In the drop-down menu, click on **Convert Text to Table**

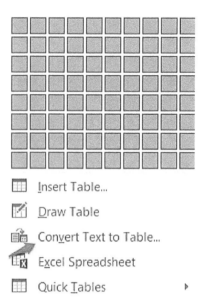

- In the **Convert Text to Table** dialog box, set the number of columns and rows, set the Autofit behavior, and separate text with either paragraph, tabs, commas, and another symbol manually assigned to it.

- Click on **Ok,** and the text will be converted to a table as shown in the image below.

ORANGE	MANGO	GUAVA	ALVOCADO	GRAPE	PINEAPLE
WATER MELON	PAWPAW	CUCUMBER	CASHEW	APPLE	

Creating a Quick Table

The Quick Table is a built-in table and it is best used if you want to insert a quick calendar, matrix, or tabular list.

To create a Quick Table, follow the procedures given below

- Go to the **Insert** tab and click on **Table** in the **Table** group

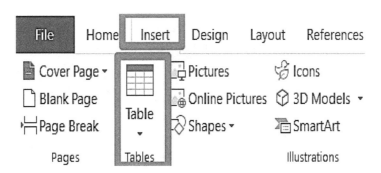

- In the drop-down menu, click on **Quick Table**

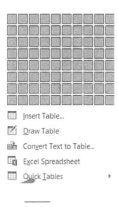

- Select any of the ready-made tables you want

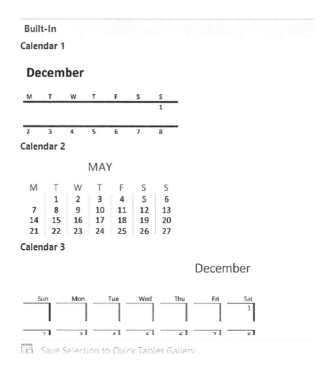

Note: *After inserting the Quick Table, you can edit and format it as like any other table created from the scratch.*

Constructing a Table from an Excel Worksheet

You can create a table from the Excel Worksheet by following the steps below:

- Go to the **Insert** tab and click on **Table** in the **Table** group

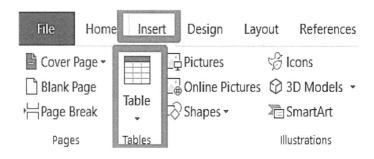

- In the drop-down menu, click on **Excel Spreadsheet.**

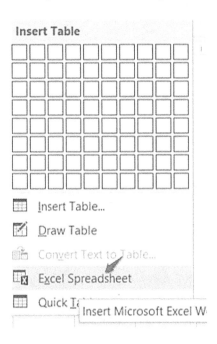

- An Excel sheet appears and the Word tabs and commands are replaced with Excel tabs and commands

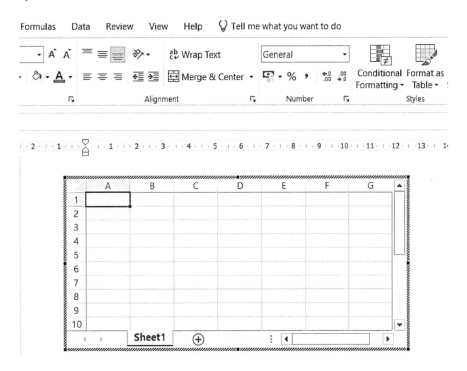

- Click outside the worksheet to return to Word. Here, the Excel worksheet is displayed in the Word document as a table

Navigating Within a Table

To move around your table, the following shortcut techniques will be of help:

Keys	Description
Tab	To move to the next column in row
Shift + Tab	To move to the previous column in a row
↓	To move to the row below
↑	To move the row above
Alt+ Home	To move to the beginning of the row
Alt + End	To move to the end of the row
Alt + Page Up	To move to the top of the column
Alt + Page Down	To move to the bottom of the column

Entering Text and Numbers in Your Tables

To enter text and numbers in your table, place the insertion point in any cell in the cell, then start typing.

Formatting Your Table

Here in this section, we will be learning how to change the customization of the table by changing the sizes of your tables, rows, and column, adding new rows or columns, deleting the rows or columns, adding table styles, borders, background, etc.

Adding Row and Columns

There are several ways to insert a new row and column into a table. Here, we will be learning two out of them.

- Using the (Table Tool) Layout Tab
- Using the Right Click

Using the (Table Tool) Layout Tab

To insert a row or column using the Layout tab, follow the steps below

- Position the cursor in the table where you wish to insert the column or row

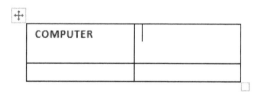

- Click on the **(Table Tool) Layout** tab and click on either **Insert Above, Insert Below, Insert Left**, or **Insert Right**.

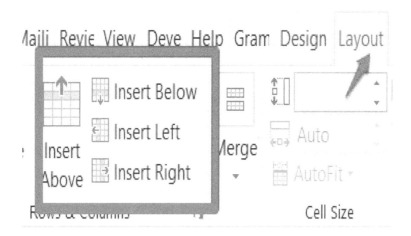

- The image below shows the result of adding rows and columns to the table

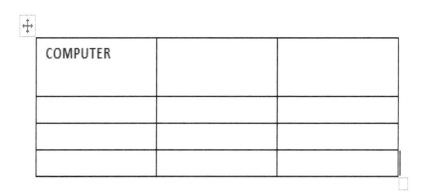

Using the Right Click

To add a row or column by using the right-click, follow the steps below

- Select the column or row
- Right-click inside the column or column and select **Insert**
- Select any of the **Insert** commands **(Insert Column to the Left, Insert Column to the Right, Insert Rows Above, or Insert Rows Below)**

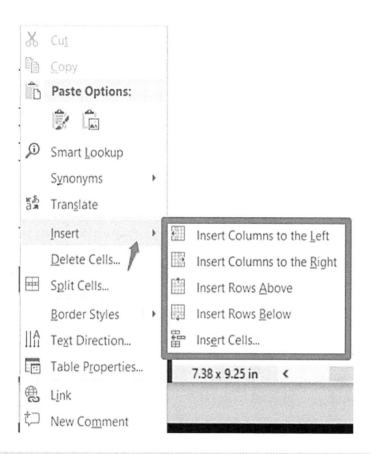

Changing the Size of Your Columns or Row

To adjust the size of your column or row, do the following

- Place the pointer onto the **Gridline**
- When the pointer turns into a double-headed arrow, drag the row or column to the desired size.

You can also adjust the size of your column or row by doing the following too

- Go to the **(Table Tools) Layout tab**, enter the measurements in the **Height and Width** text boxes. Doing this affects the columns or rows in the table

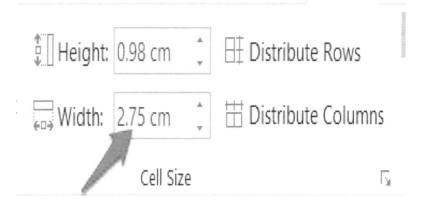

Changing the Size of Your Table

Not only can you change the size of the table, but you can also adjust the size of your table to what you want. To do this, follow the steps below

- Go to the **(Table Tools) Layout tab** and click on **Properties** under the **Table** group.

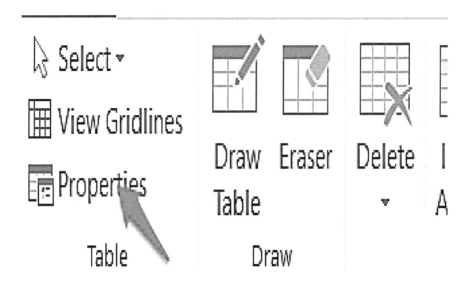

- In the **Table Properties** dialog box, enter the measurement in the **Preferred Width** text box.
- Then click on **OK**

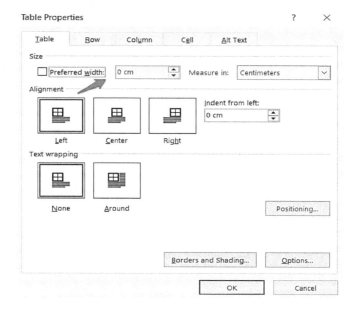

Note: You can also adjust the size of your table by dragging the top, bottom, or side of the table.

Deleting Columns and Rows

To delete the rows and columns, follow the steps below

- Position the cursor in the table where you wish to delete the column or row

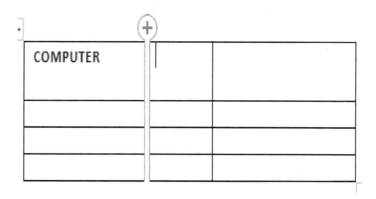

- Click on (**Table Tool**) **Layout** tab, select Delete and click on **Delete Columns** or **Delete Rows**

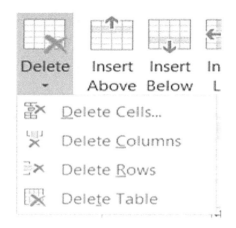

- Here, the row or column is deleted.

COMPUTER	

Aligning Texts in Columns and Rows

Aligning your text in the columns and rows of your table determines how the text will be position, whether vertically or horizontally. To align text in a table, follow the steps provided below:

- Select the cells you wish to align

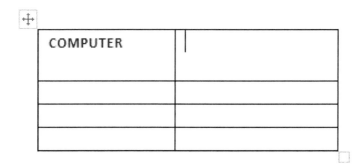

COMPUTER	TELEVISION
JOYSTICK	PROJECTOR

- Go to **(Table Tools) Layout tab**
- Click on the Alignment button, and then select any of the alignment you wish to apply to cells

- Here in the illustration below, the cells are aligned to the specific alignment you choose

COMPUTER	TELEVISION
JOYSTICK	PROJECTOR

Merging and Splitting Cells

To merge cells means to break down obstacles among cells and bring them together into one cell, while to split cells means to divide a single cell into several cells.

Merging the Cells

To merge cells, follow the steps provided below

- Select the cells you wish to merge

COMPUTER	TELEVISION
JOYSTICK	PROJECTOR

- Go to the **(Table Tools) Layout** tab and click on **the Merge Cells** button.

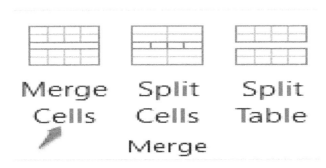

Merge Cells   Split Cells   Split Table

Merge

- In the illustration below, the cells are merged in a single cell.

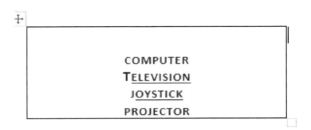

COMPUTER
TELEVISION
JOYSTICK
PROJECTOR

Splitting the Cells

To split a cell, follow the steps provided below

- Select the cell you wish to split

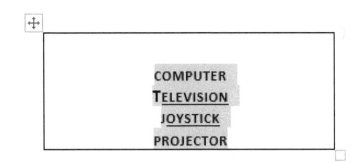

- Go to the **(Table Tools) Layout** tab and click on **the Split Cells** button.

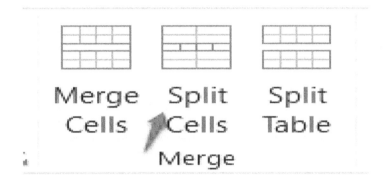

- In the **Split Cells** dialog box, enter the number of columns and columns and then click on **Ok.**

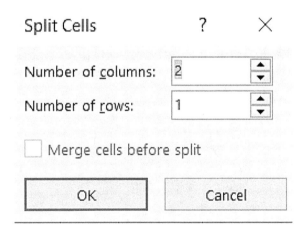

- Here, the cell is split into cells

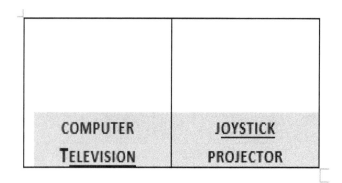

| COMPUTER | JOYSTICK |
| TELEVISION | PROJECTOR |

Sorting Data in a Table

You can sort out data in your table in either ascending or descending order. To sort out data in your data, follow the steps below:

- Place the cursor anywhere in your table

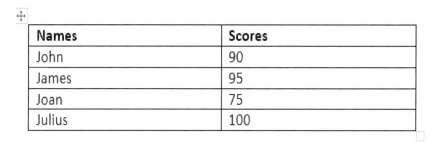

Names	Scores
John	90
James	95
Joan	75
Julius	100

- Go to **(Table Tools) Layout** tab and click on the **Sort** button under **Data** group

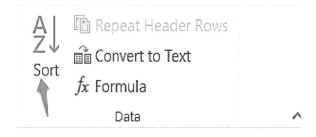

- In the **Sort** dialog box, select in ascending order, and then click on Ok

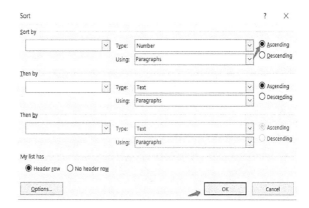

- In the table below, the data is sorted in ascending order.

Names	Scores
Joan	80
John	90
James	95
Julius	100

Applying Table Styles to Your Table

Table styles help to change the appearance of your table without changing the data. Table styles contain many design elements such as color, border, and fonts.

- To apply the styles to your table, follow the steps below:
- Click anywhere in the table, go to **(Table Tools) Design** tab

- Locate the **Table Styles** group and click on the **More** drop-down arrow to view the list of styles.

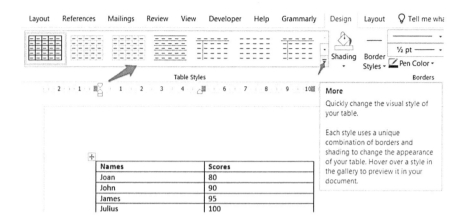

- Choose the **Table Styles** you want

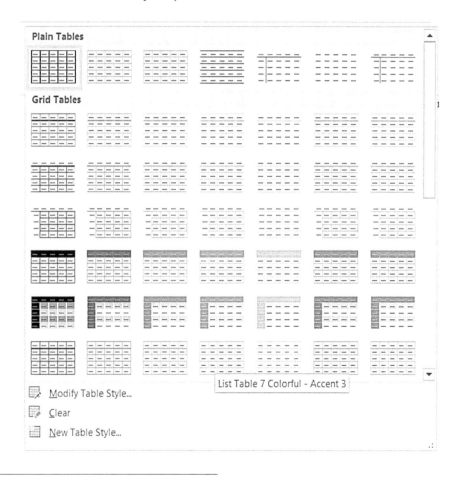

- In the table below, the table style will appear.

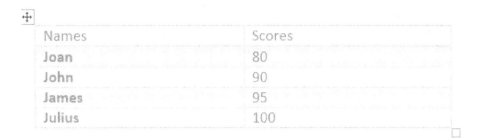

Adding Borders to Your Table

Borders allow you to add color to your columns and rows to make them have a professional look and touch.

To add a border to your table, follow the steps given below

- Go to **(Table Tools) Design** tab, click on the **Border Styles** and select the border among the list of border styles

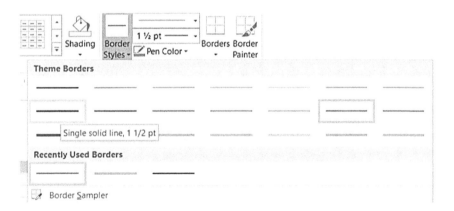

- Select where the border will be placed anywhere on the table and the table will appear with the border.

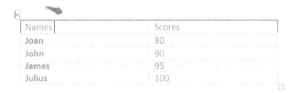

Adding Shades to Your Table

Adding shades to your table allows you to paint your tables with different colors, thus, giving your table an amazing outlook.

To add shades to your table, follow the steps below:

- Select the place you wish to shade in the table

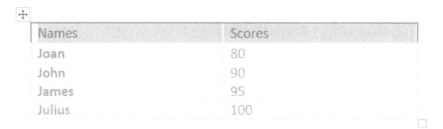

- Go to the **(Table Tools) Design** tab, click on the **Shadow** button, and then choose your desired color.

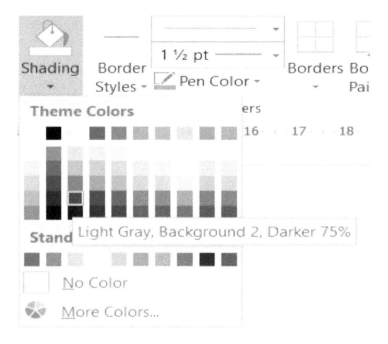

- The table appears with the shade color

Names	Scores
Joan	80
John	90
James	95
Julius	100

Wrapping Text Around Your Table

Word does not only allow you to just create tables, it allows you to wrap text around them. To wrap text around your table, follow the steps below:

- Go to the **(Table Tools) Layout** tab and click on the **Cell Size** group button.

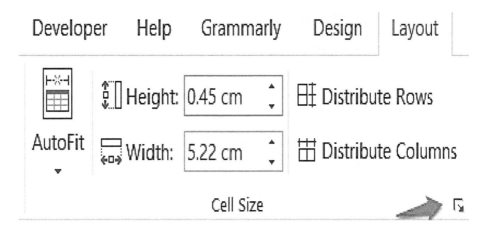

- The **Table Properties** dialog box displays. Then go to the **Table** tab and select the **Around** option under **Text Wrapping.**

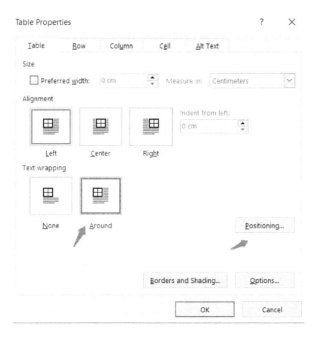

- Click on the **Positioning** button

- Select the **Move with Text** check box and click on **OK**

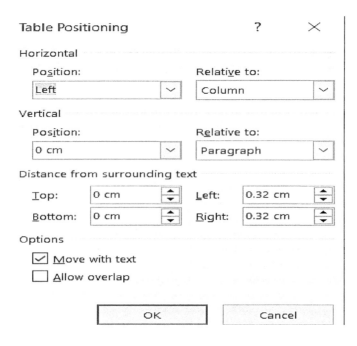

- Click **OK** in the **Table Properties** dialog box.

- Go back to the table, type the text and the text will be wrapped around the table.

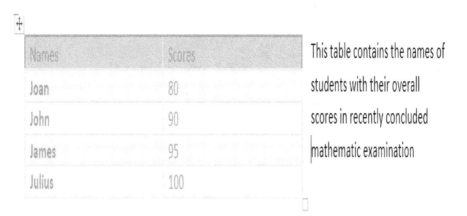

Names	Scores
Joan	80
John	90
James	95
Julius	100

This table contains the names of students with their overall scores in recently concluded mathematic examination

Applying Picture as the Table Background

To make your table look more attractive, you can add apply a picture as the background. This process may require a bit of your energy, but if you can stay through, it will be worth the effort. While trying to apply an image to your table background, you must take note of the font colors for the text in the table, so that the image can blend with text to be able to be read easily.

To insert an image as your table background, follow the steps provided below

- Place the cursor anywhere in the table

- Go to the **Insert tab**, click on **Picture** or **Online Picture** button.

- Here, we will be getting the image from the **Picture** button. In the **Picture** dialog box, locate where the image is saved, and then click on **Insert.**

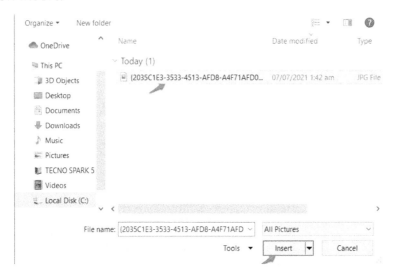

- When the image appears on the table, click on the image to locate the **Layout Option** behind the image. Click on the **Layout |Option** and choose **Behind Text** on the drop-down list.

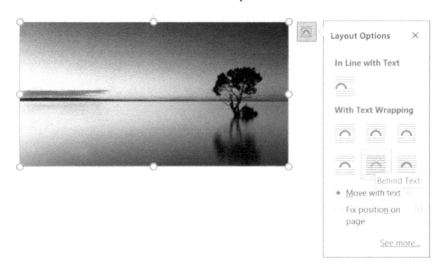

- Insert the table into the image and adjust it until it is the same size as the image

- You now enter the data, select the font and font color, select a border and border color, and align the text.

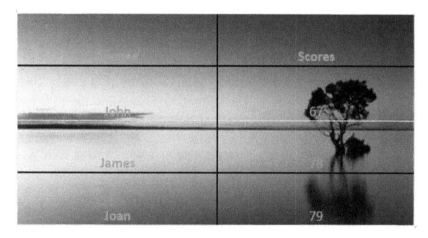

Applying Diagonal Lines on Your Table

Diagonal lines are lines that help you differentiate among cells. With diagonal lines, you can cancel out a cell from other cells.

To draw a diagonal line on your table, follow the steps given below

- Select the cells you wish to apply the diagonal line

- Go to the **(Table Tools) Design tab** and click on the **Cell Size** group button.

- Click on **Border** and choose either **Diagonal Down Border** or **Diagonal Up Border** in the drop-down list

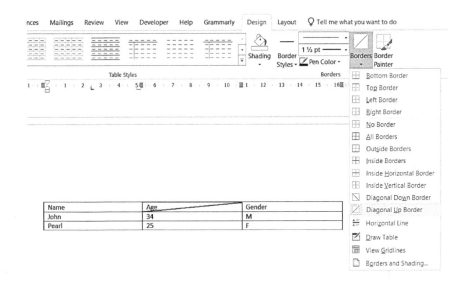

Using Mathematics Formulas in Tables

Not only can just enter text and numerical data into your table, but you can also carry out mathematical operations by using Excel formulas such as Sum, Product, Average, Count, Min, Max, etc.

Let's find the product of the data given in the table below using the following steps.

Name	Days of Absent
John	4
Pearl	2
James	5
Loveth	7
SUM TOTAL	

- Place the cursor in the cell that will contain the total of the data above.

- Go to the **(Table Tools) Layout** tab, and click on the **Formula** button.

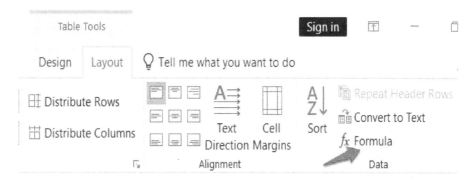

- In the **Formula** dialog box, enter the equal sign with the name of the Formula and enter either **Left, Right, Above,** or **Below** within the parenthesis in the Formula box; **=(SUMABOVE).**

- In the **Number Format** drop-down list, select the format of the number, and then click on **Ok.**

- The table below shows the total of the data.

Name	Days of Absent
John	4
Pearl	2
James	5
Loveth	7
SUM TOTAL	18

CHAPTER EIGHT

USING THE PROOFING TOOLS

No matter how perfect and flawless you are on Word 365, there will always be some unavoidable mistakes or errors, that occur around spelling and grammar. These errors can cost you more than what you can imagine especially in the business and educational world. To avoid these errors, that is why you need to make the best use of the Proofing Tools

The Proofing Tools

The proofing tools allow you to use the spelling and grammar checking features in Word for a wide range of languages to check for spelling errors and grammatical error

The proofing tool is in the **Review tab**, on the left-hand side under the **Proofing** category

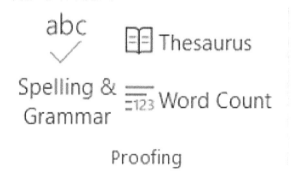

Checking for Spelling Errors in Your Documents

You can check for spelling errors in your documents by either correcting spelling errors one at a time or running a spelling check.

Correcting Spelling Errors One Step at a Time

You can correct your spelling errors without running the spell check method.

To do this:

- Locate the word that is underlined with a red line and then right-click on it

- Select the correct spelling from the **Spelling** shortcut menu

- After doing this, the word misspelled is replaced with the word you right-clicked on

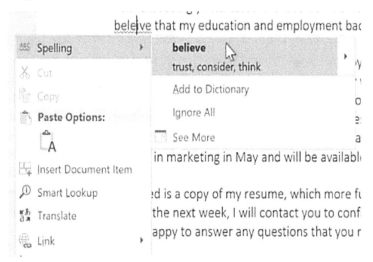

Running the Spell Check

Correcting spelling errors one by one can be a waste of time; therefore, you use the Spell check which is faster. To start your spell check, you can use any of the following methods

- Press **F7**

- Go to the **Status bar** and click on the **Proofing Error** button

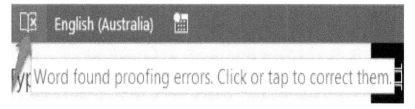

- Go to the Review tab and click on **Spelling & Grammar**

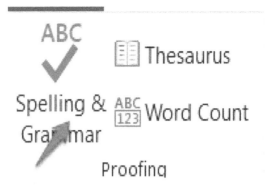

Proofing

- The Editor task pane displays where you can view the number of spellings and grammar errors in your documents.

- Click on Spelling in the task pane to see the suggestions provided for a misspelling, and then click on the correct spelling.

Preventing Text from Being Spell Checked

There are certain words in your documents that cannot be spell-checked especially words like address lists, lines of computer codes, and foreign languages such as French, Spanish, etc. To prevent text of this kind of being spell checked, follow the steps below

- Select the text.

- On the **Review tab**, click on the **Language** button, and select **Set Proofing Language.**

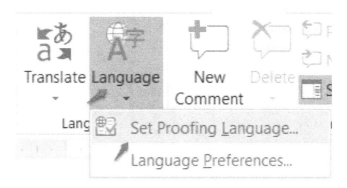

- In the **Language** dialog box, click on the **Do not check spelling or grammar** check box

Correcting Grammatical Errors

Just like how spellings are corrected, the same techniques apply to correcting grammatical errors.

Correcting Grammatical Errors One Step at a Time

You can correct grammar errors without, follow the steps below

- Locate the word that is underlined with a blue line and right-click on it

- Correct the grammatical error from the **Grammar** shortcut menu

- After doing this, the grammatical error will be replaced with the word you right-clicked on.

Correcting Grammatical Errors Using Editor Task Pane

You can use the Editor task pane to correct your grammatical errors. Primarily, you will need to open the Editor task pane. To open the Editor task pane, you any of the following methods

- Press **F7**

- Go to the **Status bar** and click on the **Proofing Error** button

- Go to the Review tab and click on **Spelling & Grammar**

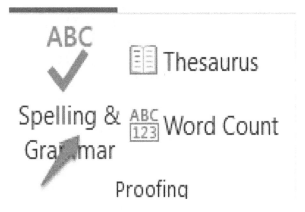

Proofing

- When the **Editor** task pane opens, select **Grammar** in the task pane and then click on the option under **Suggestions.**

Ignoring Errors

It is no doubt that the spelling and grammar check is aimed at correcting errors, yet, it is not always correct. There are several instances where Word will see some words as errors when they are not. This happens a lot when the names and other proper nouns are not included in the dictionary, especially foreign languages, or computer codes.

However, you can choose to ignore any word that is tagged to be an error by Word from the options provided by Word for both spellings and grammar check.

For Spelling errors, you can choose any of the following options

- **Ignore:** This skips the misspelled word without changing it but stops on it if the same word appears again.

- **Ignore All:** This skips the misspelled word without changing it, and it also skips the same word if it appears again.

- **Add to Dictionary:** This adds the word to the dictionary so that it will not come up as an error. Ensure that the words are correctly spelled before adding them to the dictionary.

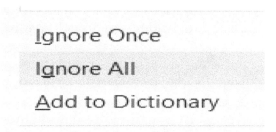

For Grammar errors, you get to choose just one option:

- **Ignore Once**: This skips the word or phrase without changing it.

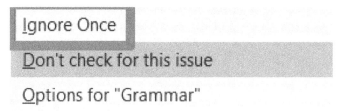

Customizing Spelling & Grammar Check

By default, there are some errors your proofing tools ignore without correcting, which you will want your proofing tools to correct.

To include all these in your spelling and grammar check, follow the steps given below

- Go to the **Backstage view** by clicking on the **File** menu

File | **Home** | Insert | Draw | Design | Layout | References | Mailings | Review | View | Developer | Help

- Click on **Options** in the left pane

- In the **Word Options** dialog box, click on **Proofing**

- On the left-hand side under **When correcting spellings and grammar in Word**, click on **Settings.**

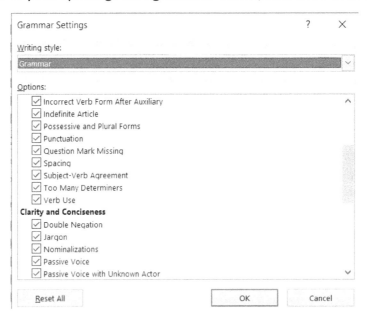

When correcting spelling and grammar in Word

- ☑ Check spelling as you type
- ☑ Mark grammar errors as you type
- ☑ Frequently confused words
- ☑ Check grammar with spelling
- ☑ Show readability statistics

Writing Style: Grammar & Refinements ▼ Settings...

Recheck Document

- In the **Grammar Settings** dialog box, select the options you wish to add to your spellings and grammar check, and then click on **Ok**

Hiding Spellings and Grammar Errors in a Document

In case you want to share your document with a person, and you do not want the person to see the red and blue lines. All you need to do is turn off the automatic spelling and grammar checks. Not only will the errors be hidden on your computer, but they also will not be displayed when viewed on another computer. To hide the spellings and grammar errors, follow the steps given below

- Go to the **Backstage view** by clicking on the **File** menu

- Click on **Options** in the left pane

- In the **Word Options** dialog box, click on **Proofing**

- Go to **Exceptions for** and click on the checkboxes; **Hide spelling error in this document only** and **Hide grammar in this document only**

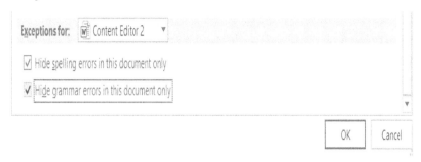

Finding and Replacing Text

While working with a longer document, it can be stressful and time-consuming to locate a word or phrase. However, Word has some features that allow such as the Find command, advanced Find command, and Find and Replace command.

Find Text Command

This allows you to use the Navigation pane to search for specific words or phrases in a document. To use this command, follow the steps given below

- Go to the **Home** tab, click on **Find** and the **Navigation pane** appears.

- In the **Search document** box in the **Navigation pane**, enter the text you wish to find.

- Use the arrows under the search box to move to **Previous** or **Next** search results.

- When you are done, click on the **X** button to close the **Navigation pane**

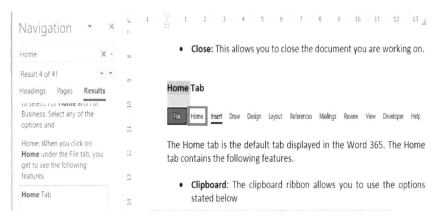

Advanced Find Command

This command allows you to search your documents for more specific items, such as match cases, wildcards, whole words, etc.

To use the Advanced Find command, follow the steps given below

- Go to the **Home** tab, click on the **Find** button list arrow and select **Advanced Find**

- In the **Find and Replace** dialog box opens, enter the word of the **Find** box.

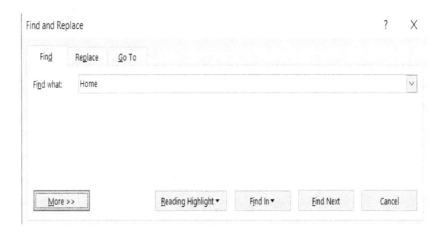

- Click on the **More** button; the More button allows you to set some options such as Match case, Wildcards, Match prefix, etc. on how to search.

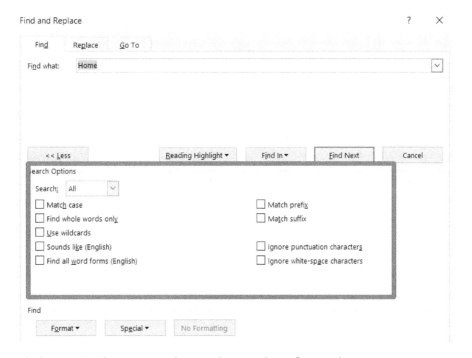

- Click on **Find Next** and Word searches from the current cursor location to the end of the document. If you click on **Find All**, Word searches the entire document.

- Then click on **Close** at the top of the dialog box.

The Replace Command

The Replace command allows you to find any word in your document and replace it with another. This can come in handy when you have misspelled a word in many places, and you wish to correct it. To use the Replace command, follow the steps given below

- Go to the **Home** tab, click on **Replace**

- In the **Find and Replace** dialog box, open the **Replace t**ab

- Enter the word you need to find in the **Find what** text field

- Enter the word you want to replace within the **Replace with** text field

- Select any of the replacement options.

  ○ **Replace**: This replaces individual instances of the text.

  ○ **Replace All**: This replaces every instance of the text in the entire document.

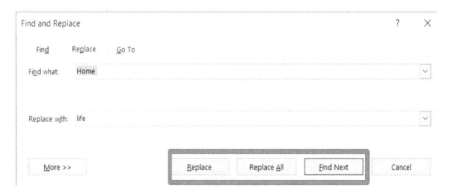

- Click on **Ok**

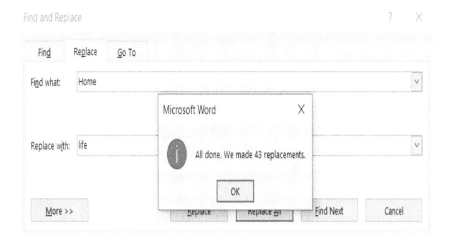

- Then Press **Close** when you are done

Getting the Right Words with Thesaurus

The Thesaurus is a software tool in a Microsoft Word document that allows you to look for synonyms and antonyms of selected words.

There are three ways to open and use the Thesaurus:

- Press Shift + F7

- Right-click on any word, select **Synonyms** and then click on **Thesaurus**

... the The...rus:

...s, and then click on Thesaurus

- Go to the **Review** tab, and click on the **Thesaurus** button

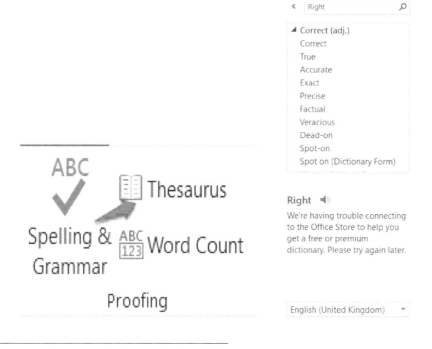

Proofing Text Written in Foreign Language

Apart from English Language, Word allows you to make use of foreign languages such as Uzbek, Spanish, Estonian, etc. You can check spell text written in these languages. To use these foreign languages in your document, follow the steps given below

- Go to the **Review tab**, click on the **Language** button and select the **Language Preferences**.

- In the dialog box that appears, Open the **Add Additional Languages** drop-down list, select any language of your choice, and then click on **Add** to include the language in your document

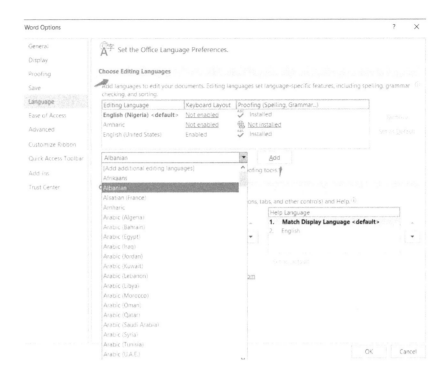

- Click on **Ok** and a message box will display telling you to restart Office for the changes to take effect.

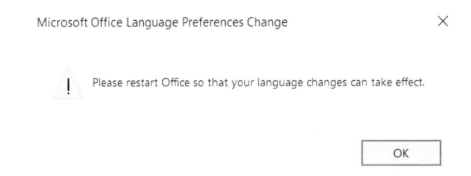

Marking Text as Foreign Language Text

Marking your text as a foreign language text notifies Office where in your document you are using a foreign language. With this, Office can spell-check the text using the proper dictionary.

To mark text as a foreign language, follow the steps given below

- Select the text written in a foreign language

- Go to the **Review** tab, click on the **Language** button, and select **Set Proofing Language** in the drop-down list.

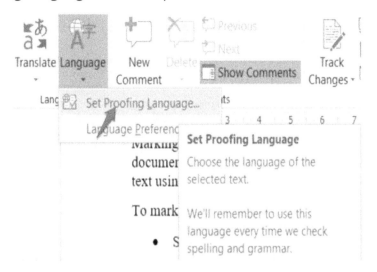

- In the **Language** dialog box, select a language and click on **Ok**

Translating Foreign Language

You do not have to worry about working on a document in a foreign language any longer, Why? Office provides the Translator which is used for translating words and phrases from one language to another. To translate a document from one language to another, follow the steps given below

- Select the word or phrases you wish to translate

Merci d'être venu à ma fête

- Go to the **Review** tab, click on the **Translate** button, and select any of the **Translate** options

  - **Translate Selection:** This opens the Translator task pane and translates the selected word or phrases with Microsoft Translator.

  - **Translate Document:** This opens the Translator task pane and creates a translated copy of your document with Microsoft Translator.

NOTE: To use the Translator, you must have a strong internet connection

DESKTOP PUBLISHING WITH WORD

Gone are those days when all you could do with a word processor is to type and make some formatting on your documents. Over the years, Microsoft Word has taken a new turn, by having some basic features with a desktop publisher.

In this part of this book, you will be learning how to apply some desktop publishing features such as themes, watermark, drop caps, etc.

Using Themes on Your Document

A theme is a set of colors, fonts, and effects applied to a document to determine the outlook of such document. Applying themes to your document helps to easily change its appearance.

Choosing A New Theme

To choose or apply a new theme to your document, follow the steps given below

- Go to the **Design** tab and click on **Theme t**o choose any of the themes you desire on the drop-down list

Choosing a New Style Set

To choose a new style set, follow the steps below

- Go to the **Design** tab and click on the **Theme Style Set gallery t**o choose any of the style set you desire on the drop-down list.

Document Formatting

Choosing a New Set of Colors for Your Themes

To choose a new set of colors for your themes

- Go to the **Design** tab and click on the **Theme Colors** button

- Move the pointer to select any color from the drop-down list.

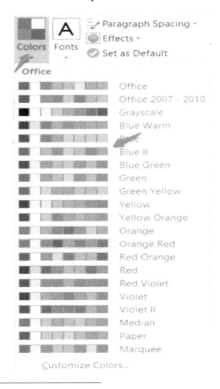

Changing the Fonts

To choose the theme font for your document, follow the steps below

- Go to the **Design** tab, click on **Theme font**, and select any of the fonts you want from the drop-down list

Dressing Up Your Pages

Here in this part of this book, we shall be learning how to design the pages of your document by putting a border around pages, applying colors on pages, and lots more.

Decorating the Page of Your Document with Border

With Word 365, you can decorate the title page, certificate, and other related documents with the page border.

To apply a border to your document, follow the steps given below:

- Move the cursor to where you wish to insert the border

- Go to the **Design** tab and click on the **Page Borders** button

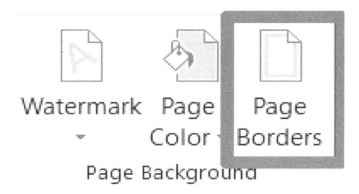

- In the **Borders and Shading** dialog box, click on the **Page Border** tab

- under **Settings** select the kind of border you want

- Click on **Style** to select the lines of the border; Solid, Dotted, or Dashed.

- Click on **Artwork** to display how wide the lines or artwork should be

- On the **Apply To** drop-down menu, select the page or pages in the document to insert the borders.

- Click on the **Options** button to know how close know the borders can come to the edge of the page or pages.

- Click on the four buttons in the **Preview** window to remove or add borders on your page.

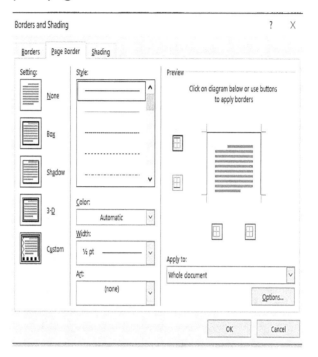

- Then click on **Ok** to see the border inserted on the page

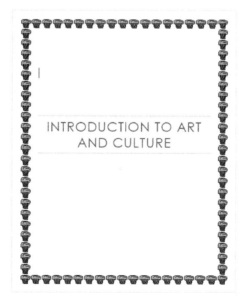

Adding a Background Color to Your Page

You can add a background color to your page by following the steps below

- Go to the **Design** tab, click on the **Page Colors** button, and select any color in the drop-down list.

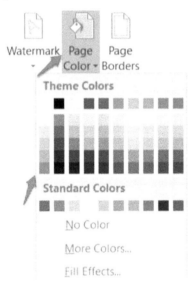

- To apply gradient color or mixtures or patterns to the pages, click on **Fill Effect** and select any gradient color from the **Fill Effects** dialog box.

- The image below shows the page with background-color

Getting Word 365 Help with Cover Letters

There are instances you will be needing cover letters for your letters, resume, or report. With Word 365, you can get a good and well-preformatted cover letter that will fit in with your report or article.

To insert a cover page at the front of your document

- Go to the **Insert** tab, click on the **Cover Page** button, and select a cover page from the gallery.

Applying Charts, Diagrams, Shapes, and Photos to Your Documents.

Just like the other versions of Offline Word, Word 365 allows you to insert charts, diagrams, and photos on your document to look more refined and professional.

Inserting Chart in Your Document

A chart is a graphical representation of data. With the use of charts, you can see the result of data to have a better understanding and ability to predict current and future data. Examples of charts are bar charts, pictograms, histograms, pie charts, line charts, etc.

To insert charts in your document, follow the steps given below

- Go to the **Insert** tab and click on **Chart** on the **Illustration** group

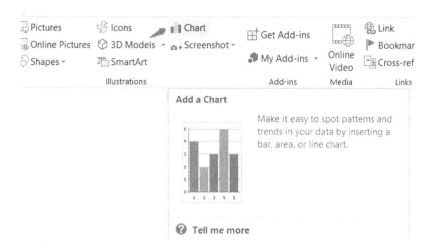

- In the **Insert Chart** dialog box, select any chart you want under **All Charts**

- Then click on **Ok.**

Inserting Diagrams in Your Document

A diagram is a symbolic representation of data using visualization techniques. Word can use diagrams to clarify concepts, explain processes and display hierarchical relationships, especially in business documents.

To insert diagrams in your document, follow the steps given below

- Go to the **Insert** tab and click on **SmartArt** on the **Illustration** group

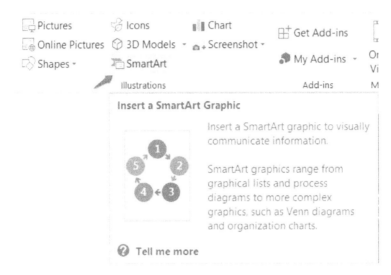

- In the **Choose a SmartArt Graphic**, select any diagram from the list.

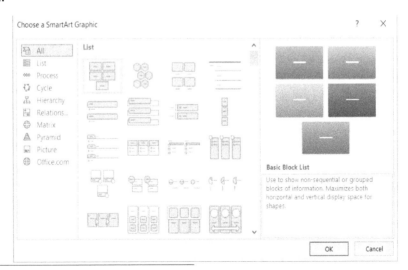

- Then click on **Ok**

Inserting Shapes in Your Documents

Shapes in Word are used to graphically display ideas and concepts. Examples of shapes are arrows, callouts, squares, stars, and flowchart shapes.

To insert shape to your document, follow the steps below

- Go to the **Insert** tab and click on **Shapes** under **Illustration** group

- In the drop-down list, select the desired shape

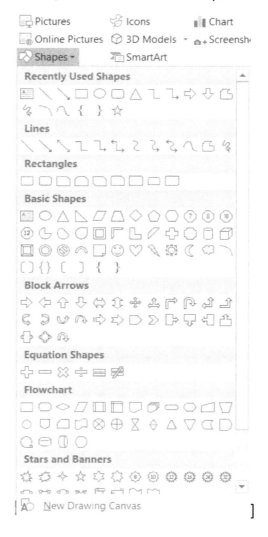

- Click and drag in the location you want to add the shape to your document.

- Once the shape has been added to your document, you can double click and drag your mouse to the edge of the shape to make it more visible.

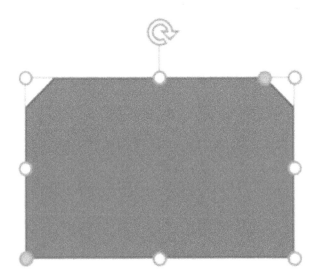

- To change the shape style, select the shape, click on **Format**, click on **More** drop-menu in the **Shape Styles**, and then select the Style you wish to use.

- The shape appears in the selected style

Inserting Picture in Your Document

To insert a picture into your document, follow the steps below

- Go to the **Insert tab**, click on the **Picture** button under **Illustration.**

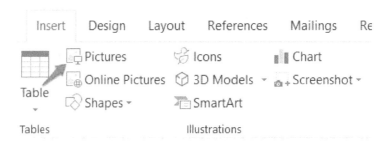

- In the **Picture** dialog box, locate where the image is saved, and then click on **Insert.**

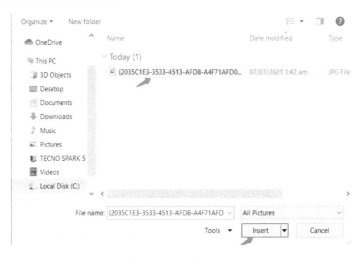

- Here the image is displayed in the document

Wrapping Text Around Image

Word 365 allows you to join words and images together to explain a document. This is made possible by wrapping text around your image.

To wrap text around an image, follow the steps below:

- Select the image you wish to wrap text around

- Click on the **Format** menu that appears at top of the Word's ribbon and selects **Wrap text.**

- Select any of the following in the **Warp Text** drop-down list

  - **Square:** Choose this option if your image is square, and you wish to wrap the text around the square border of your image.

  - **Top and Bottom:** Select this option if you want your image to stay on its own line, but between text on the top and button.

- **Tight:** Select this option if you wish to wrap text around a round or irregular-shaped image.

- **Through:** This option helps to customize the areas that the text will wrap. This is best used if you want to join the text with your image, and you do not wish to follow the line of your border.

- **Behind Text:** This option allows you to use the image as a watermark behind the text.

- **In Front of Text:** Select this option if you wish to display the image over the text. You can change the color, or make the text illegible.

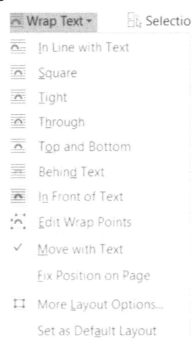

Positioning an Object on a Page

Positioning an object determines where the object will appear on the page. Automatically, the text will be wrapped around the object, so the texts can be easily read.

To position an image, follow the steps below

- Select the image you wish to position

- Click on the **Format** menu that appears at top of the Word's ribbon and select **Position Object.**

- Select an option in the **Position Object** drop-down list

Working with Text Box

 A text box is an object in Word 365 that allows you to put and type text anywhere in your document. Text boxes can be used to attract attention to a particular text and can be used to move text from one place to another in the document. You can also change the text boxes and the text within them using a variety of styles and effects.

Inserting a Text Box

You can insert a text box in a document using two methods

- By inserting a built-in text box
- By drawing a text box

Inserting a Built-in Text Box

To insert a built-in text box in a document, follow the steps below

- Go to the **Insert** tab and click on the **Text Box** command in the **Text** group

- In the **Text box** drop-down menu, select any of the text boxes

- When the selected text box appears on the document, delete the highlighted text.

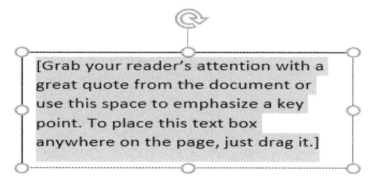

- After deleting the highlighted text, type in the text you desire

```
CULTURAL VALUE
```

Drawing Text Box

You can also insert a text box into a document by drawing a text box, to do this, follow the steps below

- Go to the **Insert** tab and click on the **Text Box** command in the **Text** group

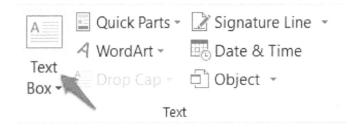

- In the **Text box** drop-down menu, select any of the text boxes

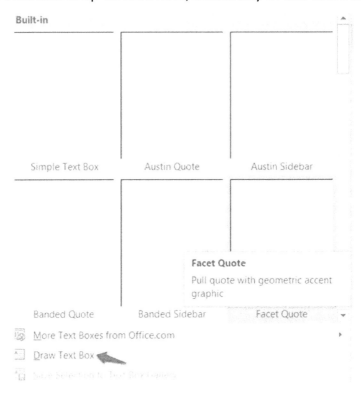

- Click and drag anywhere on the document to create the text box

- When the insertion point appears inside the text box, type the words you desire inside it.

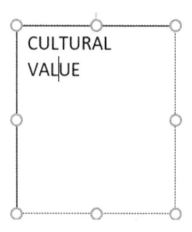

Resizing a Text Box

To resize a text box, follow the steps below

- Click on the text box you wish to resize

- Click and drag any of the sizings handles on the corners of the text box until it is adjusted to the size you want

Moving a Text Box

You can move a text box from one location to another, to do this, follow the steps below

- Click on the text box you wish to move

- Move the mouse over one of the edges of the text box and wait until it changes into a cross with arrows

- Then click and drag the text box to the desired location.

Modifying Text Boxes

Word 365 allows you to change the way your text boxes appear in the document by changing their shape, style, and color.

Changing the Shape Style of Your Text Box

To change the shape style of your text box, follow the steps given below

- Select the text box you wish to change

- Go to the **Format** tab, click on **More** drop-down list in the **Shape Styles** group

- In the **Styles** drop-down menu, select the styles you want

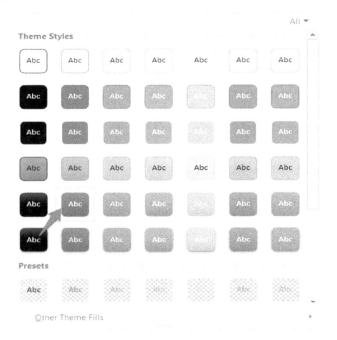

- The text box will be displayed in the selected style.

Changing the Text Box Shape

Not only can you change the style color of your text box, but you can also change the shape of your text box to any shape of your choice. To change the shape of your text, follow the steps given below

- Select the text box you wish to change

- Go to the **Format** tab and click on the **Edit Shape** command

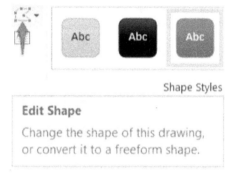

Click on **Change Shape** and select the shape you want from the **Change Shape** drop-down menu

- The text box will be displayed in the shape selected.

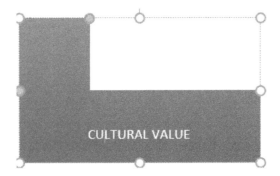

Using the Drop Cap

A drop Cap is short for dropped initial capital letter, which is a large, oversized, and single capital letter that usually appears at the start of chapters in a book.

To add a drop cap to your document, follow the steps given below

- Select the first character of the paragraph

Word 365 is a word processing application among all other applications in the Office 365 line of subscription services offered by Microsoft, to provide the users with the ability to create professional-quality documents, reports.

- Go to the **Insert tab** and click on **Drop Cap**

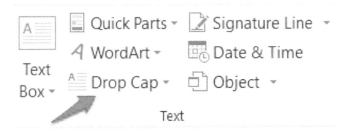

- Select the drop cap you want
  - o **Dropped:** This creates a drop cap that fits within a paragraph

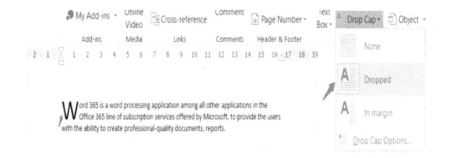

- **In Margin:** This creates a drop cap that is in the margin, and not inside the paragraph.

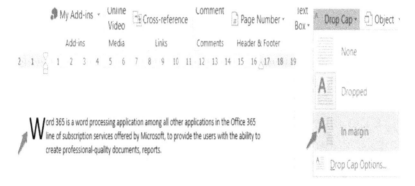

- In the **Drop Cap** dialog box, set the following options

  - **Position**: This option allows you to choose the kind of drop cap you want

  - **Font**: This option allows you to choose any kind of font to use as a text in the paragraph.

  - **Lines to Drop:** This option allows you to enter the number of text lines to drop the letter, or how high the letter will be.

  - **Distance from Text**: This option defines how much space you want to allow around the Drop Cap.

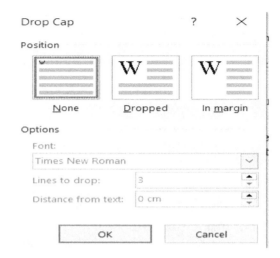

- Then click on **OK**

Using the Watermark

A watermark is a faded background image that displays behind the text in a document. Watermark can be used to specify a document's state (confidential, draft, etc.), insert company logo, etc.

Inserting Watermark

To insert a watermark in your document, follow the procedures below

- Go to the **Design** tab and click on **Watermark**

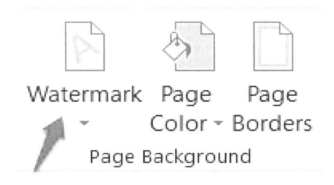

- On the **Watermark** drop-down list, select any watermark of your choice

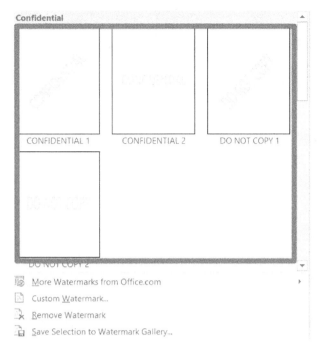

- The watermark will appear in the document

Inserting Custom Text Watermark

Custom text watermark involves you creating your own watermark using text. To do this, follow the steps given below

- Go to the **Design** tab and click on **Watermark**

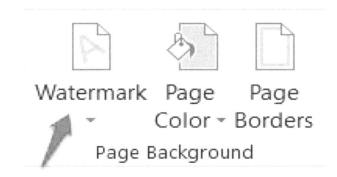

- On the **Watermark** drop-down list, select **Custom Watermark**

- In the Printed Watermark dialog box, go to **Text watermark** and set the following options.

  o **Languages**: This allows you to set the language of the text to be written in the watermark.

  o **Text**: This is the string of text that will appear in the document.

  o **Font**: This option allows you to choose any kind of font to use as a text in the paragraph.

  o **Size**: This option allows you to set the size of the text to either big or small

  o **Color**: This option allows you to change the color of your text.

  o **Layout:** This allows you to set the position of the text to either diagonal or horizontal.

  o **Semitransparent**: This option allows you to make the text visible or not visible

- Click on **Apply** and then press **OK**

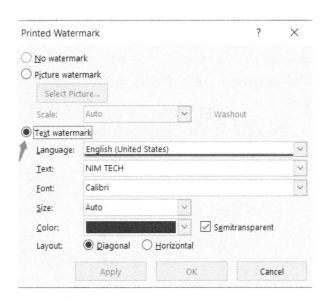

- The text watermark will appear in the document

Inserting Custom Picture Watermark

You can also display an image watermark on your document by using the custom picture watermark. To use the custom picture watermark, follow the steps below

- Go to the **Design** tab and click on **Watermark**

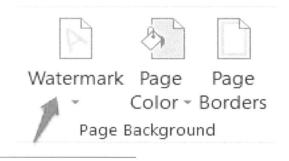

- On the **Watermark** drop-down list, select **Custom Watermark**

- In the Printed Watermark dialog box, go to **Picture watermark** and click on **Select Picture**

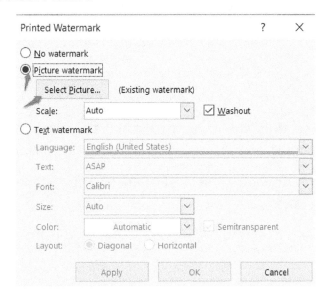

To add a picture from your drive, select the **Browse** option next to the **From a file** icon. Then navigate to the location of the image

- On the **Insert Picture** dialog box, select the picture and click on **Insert**

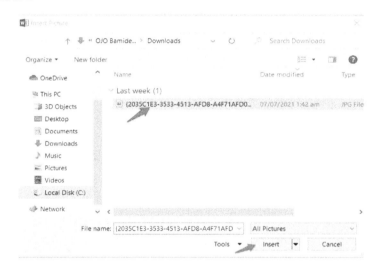

- In the Scale drop-down menu, set the size of the image selected.

- Tick the **Washout** option to make the watermark almost fully transparent, and uncheck it to make the watermark more visible.

- Click on **Apply** for the watermark to appear and **Ok** to close the dialog box.

- The picture watermark will appear in the document

Applying Newspaper Columns in Your Documents

Some data in Word are best viewed in columns. Columns in Word helps to advance readability, especially when dealing with documents such as newspapers articles, flyers, newsletters, etc.

To add columns to your document, follow the steps below

- Go to the **Layout** tab, and click on **Columns** in the **Page Setup** ribbon

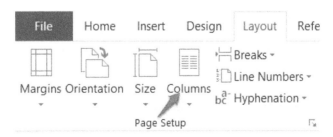

- In the Columns drop-down menu, select any column of your choice

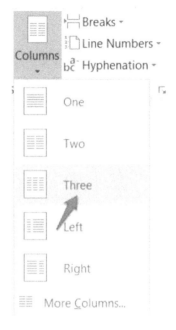

- The document appears in the selected column

There is no doubt that Office 365 and the traditional Office Suite have so many similarities. Despite all these similarities, Office 365 has some exclusive features that make it different from the traditional Office suite. However, these features are the major factors that will intrigue you to use Office 365. Now let us highlight them.

- **Easy Access from Anywhere:** Office 365 allows you to access your file anytime and anywhere using an internet connection, from any device. The Office 365 runs in a Microsoft data center, which allows the users to connect to the internet to access the software.

- **SharePoint:** One of the advantages of using Office 365 is that it allows you to use **SharePoint Online.** Using this service allows you to share and collaborate with others. To view the document by anyone in the organization, this service set up security permission.
- **Software Update:** Another advantage to the use of Office 365 is that it allows the users to get a frequent software update. These updates allow access to the latest features such as security updates, and bug fixes.

- **Secured Cloud Storage:** Office 365 has a secure working environment with high-security measures set in place such as two-factor authentication, which obstructs any authorized people to gain access to your files even while on your devices. With this in place, your confidential files are secured without any security threat or breach.

- Click on **More Columns** to open the **Column** dialog box and see the following options
    - o **Preset Columns**: This allows you to choose the preset number of columns

- ○ **Number of Columns**: This allows you to enter the number of columns you want in the document.

- ○ **Line Between Columns:** This allows you to run lines between columns.

- ○ **Columns Width:** This allows you to change the width of each column by using width boxes.

- ○ **Space Between Columns:** This determines how much space appears between columns.

- ○ **Start New Column:** This check box allows you to insert space in a column

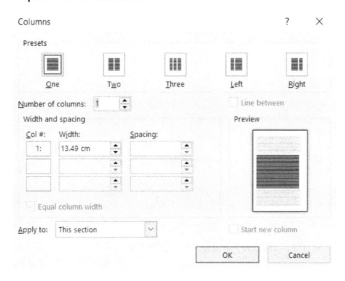

Page Orientation

Page orientation is the way elements or contents appear on a page. Word has two-page orientations which are Landscape and Portrait. Landscape means the page is oriented horizontally, while portrait means the page is oriented vertically.

Changing Page Orientation

To change the page orientation, follow the steps given below

- Go to the **Layout tab** and click on **Orientation**

- In the drop-down menu, click on either **Portrait or Landscape** to change the page orientation.

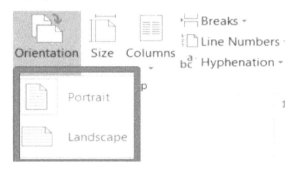

Printing on Different Size Paper

The standard 8.5 x 11 paper is not the paper size you can print on, there are other sizes of paper you can print with. To print your document in different paper sizes, follow the steps below

- Go to the **Layout** and click on **Size** in the **Page Setup** group

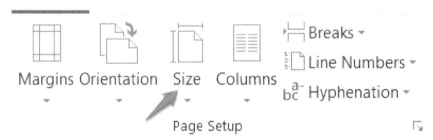

- In the **Size** drop-down menu, select any of the paper sizes you want.

Displaying Online Video in a document

Not only can you view images in your document, but you can also view videos in your document. To do this follow the steps below

- Go to the **Insert** tab and click on the **Online Video** button

- Enter the name of the video to search in the **Search YouTube** text box and click on **Enter.**

Insert Video

YouTube
Terms of Use, Privacy Policy.

From a Video Embed Code
Paste the embed code to insert a video from a web
site

Paste embed code here

- Select the video you like and click on Insert

- Enter the embed code of the video on the internet on the **Paste Embed Code Here** and then press **Enter**

CHAPTER TEN

GETTING WORD'S HELP WITH OFFICE CHORES

In this chapter, we will be learning some techniques that will help in the usage of Word 365. This involves how to highlight part of a document, adding a comment to the document, tracking changes in documents, etc,

Highlighting Part of a Document

Using the Highlight command allows you to mark certain paragraphs and text in your document that may need to be referred to later in the future.

To use the Highlight command, follow the steps below

- Select the text you wish to highlight

> People collaborating on a document can write comments and in so doing prove that two heads are better than one. Comments give you the opportunity to suggest improvements, plead with your collaborators, debate your editor, and praise others, all in the interest of turning out a better document

- Go to the **Home** tab and click on **Text Highlighter Color**. The text appears with selected text highlighted color.

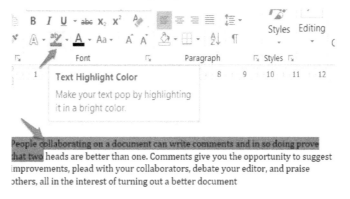

- You can also highlight a part of your document by selecting the highlighter and then click on the text.

Using Comments on a Document

The comment command is an essential part of Word 365 that allows a user to easily and effectively collaborate and make suggestions with other users on a document draft. Here, you will be learning how to insert a comment, delete comments, view comments, and lots more.

To insert a comment in your document, follow the steps below

- Select the text you wish to add the comment on

- Go to the **Review** tab and click on **New Comment**

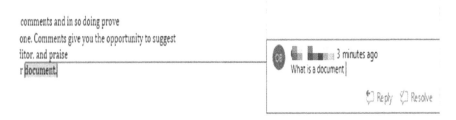

- Type in your comment in the field that is displayed at the right margin. This comprises your name and the timestamp visible for all to see.

- To edit the comment, click on the comment box and make a change.

Replying a Comment

To reply to a comment, go to the comment that needs to be replied to, click on the **Reply link**. When your name appears in the balloon so that you can enter the reply in the comment box.

Resolving a Comment

To resolve a comment, open the comment, and click on the **Resolve link**. This changes the comment to a gray color. To resume the comment, click on the **Reopen link.**

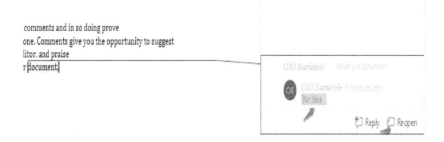

Deleting Comments

To delete the comment in your document, follow the steps given above

- Select the comment

- Go to the **Review** tab click on **Delete Comment**

- In the **Delete Comment** drop-down**,** click on **Delete**, Delete **All Section shown**, or **Delete All Comments in Documents**.

Moving Around from One Comment to Another

To move from one comment to another, go to the **Review** tab and then select click on **Previous** button or **Next** button

Tracking Changes to Documents

The Track Changes command allows you to make changes that can easily be spotted or identified. These changes can be reviewed, removed, or be made permanent. Changes made in a document are recorded in different colors, with one color for each reviewer, new text is underlined, and deleted text is crossed out.

Turning Track Changes On and Off

To turn on the track changes, follow the steps below

- Go to the **Review tab** and click on **Track Changes** to turn it on. The **Track Changes** button will appear darker than the rest of the ribbons when turned on.

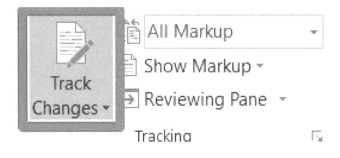

- To turn off the **Track Changes**, click on the button again. When the Track Changes is off, Word stops marking changes, but the colored underlines and strikethrough from the changes remain in the documents until they are accepted or rejected.

How to Show and Hide Track Changes

The Display for Review and Show Markup menus control how comments and edits appear

The Display for Review Menu

The Display for Review menu chooses how edits and comments are to be displayed in the document,

To locate the **Display for Review** menu, go to the **Review** tab and click on **Display for Review.**

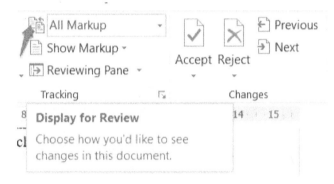

To see how edits and comments are displayed, click on the **Display for Review** drop-down menu and the options are

- **Simple Markup**: This option displays the changes made on the document with a vertical line as an indication, in the left margin.

- **All Markup**: This displays all edits and comments made in the document. new text is underlined, and deleted text is crossed out.

- **No Markup:** This displays the edited version of the document without showing any trace of visible edits or comments.

- **Original:** This displays the original version of the document without any edit or comment.

The Show Markup Menu

The **Show Markup** menu allows you to choose the features the Track Changes display

To locate the **Show Markup** menu, go to the **Review** tab and click on **Show Markup**

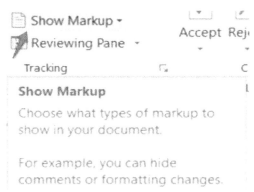

To display all comments and edits in your document, select **Show Only Comments and Formatting in Balloons**

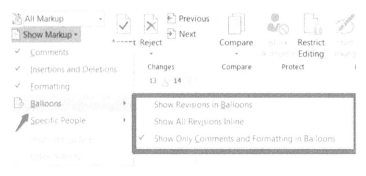

Deleting Text with Track Changes

To delete a text with Track Changes, follow the steps below

- Select the text you wish to delete

- Select the **Delete** key on the keyboard. The deleted text will appear with a strikethrough in the All Markup view.

> ~~Office 365 which was launched in 2001, was the first cloud application of Microsoft Office~~ and generates applications, services, and data hosted in Microsoft's servers.

Inserting Text with Track Changes

To insert text with Track Changes, follow the steps below

- Place the cursor where you wish to insert the new text

- Type the new text, and the new text will appear with an underline

> Office 365 which was launched in 2001, was the first could application of Microsoft Office and generates application, services, and data hosted in Microsoft's services

Replacing Text with Track Changes

To replace text with track changes, follow the steps below

- Select the text you wish to replace

- Type the replacement text and the original text will appear with a strikethrough. While the replacement text will appear with an underline in the All Markup view.

Before Word 365 came into existence, there are have been several versions of Microsoft Word being used. Quickly, we will be highlighting the versions of Microsoft Word up to date.

~~Word 365 is a word processing application among all other applications in the Office 365 line of subscription services offered by Microsoft.~~

Changing Formatting with Track Changes

Formatting your document involves applying font style, font size, font color, italics, etc.

To format text, follow the steps below

- Select the text you wish to format

- Change the format and the Track Changes will automatically show the selected formatting applied in the document

Accept or Reject Track Changes

Changes made with Track Changes must be accepted before they become part of the document. You can either accept or reject edits individually or all at once.

To accept or reject track changes, select the change made, go to the **Review** tab, and do any of the following

- **Accept a change**: Click the **Accept** button or open the drop-down list on the **Accept** button and select **Accept This Change** or **Accept and Move to Next.**

- **Reject a change:** Click the **Reject** button or open the drop-down list on the **Reject** button and select **Reject Change** or **Reject and Move to Next.**

- **Accept all changes:** Open the drop-down list on the **Accept** button and select **Accept All Changes.**

- **Reject all changes**: Open the drop-down list on the **Reject** button and select **Reject All Changes.**

CHAPTER ELEVEN

WORKING WITH TOOLS FOR REPORTS AND SCHOLARLY PAPERS

This chapter is focused explicitly on writing reports, manuals, and scholarly ease by learning how to generate a table of contents, creating footnotes and endnotes, creating an index, and lots more.

Alphabetizing a List

In case you need to arrange some words in a list on your document in alphabetical order, the Sort By command got you covered. To alphabetize a list, follow the steps given below

- Select the list you wish to arrange alphabetically

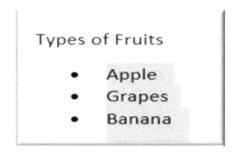

- Go to the **Home** tab and click on the **Sort** button

- In the Sort Text dialog box, click on Ok and the list will be arranged alphabetically.

Types of Fruits

- Apple
- Banana
- Grapes|

Collapsing and Expanding the Parts of Your Document

Collapsing and expanding the parts of your documents allows you to hide and show certain parts of your document. Before you can collapse and expand some parts of your document, the document must have headings styles (Heading 1, Heading 2, Heading 3, etc.)

To collapse or expand certain parts of the documents, move the pointer over a heading and click on the Collapse or Expand button.

Navigating Your Document Using the Table of Content

A table of content is just like a compass to getting anywhere within the book. A book no matter good it is is not complete without a table of content.

A table of contents is a list of chapters or headings at the beginning of a book, containing the page numbers of each chapter or heading, and starting where each chapter or heading is located within the documents.

Using a table of content in your document gives you the following benefits:

- Creating a table of content gives a bird's eye view of the document i.e., you get to see how the document flows from one topic to the next with just a glance.

- Creating a table of content in your document gives it a professional look.

- A table of content makes a document easier to discuss.

- A table of content gives the reader a learning path on any subject of his choice.

Creating a Table of Content

Creating a table of content is easier than you think. To create a table of content, follow the steps given below

Select the text you want to apply heading to in your document and apply a heading style to

- Go to the **Home** tab, and select the desired headings in the **Style** group

- After applying the heading styles, position the cursor where you want the table of content to be

- Go to the **Reference** tab and click on the **Table of Content** button. Select a built-in table from the menu that appears, and the table of content will appear in your document.

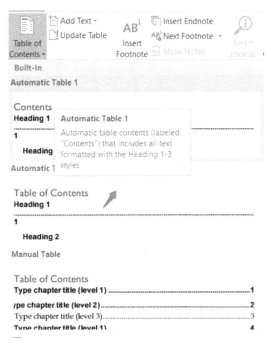

Updating Your Table of Content

In case you add, remove, or edit a heading in your document, you will need to update your table of content to take effect. Follow the steps below to update your table of content:

- Go to the **Reference** tab and click on the **Update Table** button.

- Click on **Update Entire Table** and press on **OK**

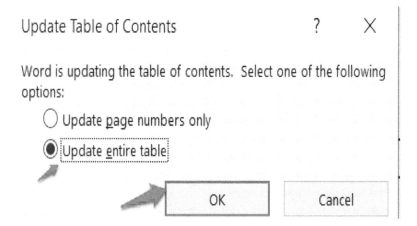

Note: You can also select the table of content and click on **Update Table**

Removing Table of Content

To remove the table of content, do the following:

- Go to the **Reference** tab, click on **Table of Content**, and select **Remove Table of Content** on the drop-down list.

Customizing Your Table of Content

Apart from using the built-in table of contents, you can create a table of contents that matches what you want by using the Customize Table of Content Command.

To customize your table of content, follow the steps given below

- Go to the **Reference** tab, click on **Table of Content**, and select **Customize Table of Content** on the drop-down list.

 More Tables of Contents from Office.com

 Custom Table of Contents...

 Remove Table of Contents

 Save Selection to Table of Contents Gallery...

- In the **Table of Content** dialog box, choose the following options to set the headings and how they should be formatted.

  - **Showing Page Numbers:** This option allows you to deselect the Show Page Numbers box if you want the table of content to be a simple list that does not refer to the headings by page.

  - **Align the Page Numbers:** This option allows you to select the Right Align Page Numbers check box if you want the page numbers to line up along the right side of the Table of content.

  - **Choosing a Table Leader:** This allows you to choose the leader to apply.

  - **Choosing a Format:** This allows you to choose from the Formats drop-down list.

  - **Choosing a Table of Content Depth:** This option determines the number of headings included in the table of content.

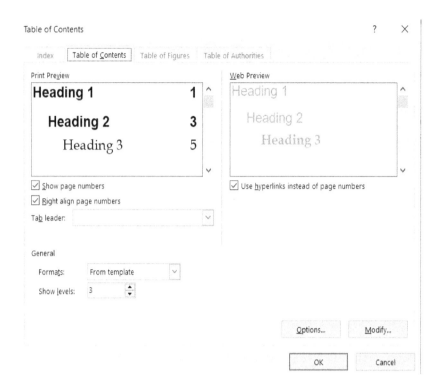

Indexing a Document

An index makes an outline or list of topics that are discussed in a document and the pages where they can be found. To create an index, you must mark the index entries by providing the name of the main entry and the cross-reference in your documents, and then you build the index.

Marking the Entries in Your Document

To mark entries in your document, follow the steps below

- Select the text you wish to use as an index entry

- Go to the **Reference** tab, and click on the **Mark Entry** in the **Index group.**

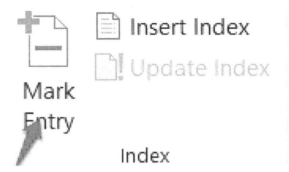

- In the **Mark Index Entry** dialog, the selected text will appear in the Main Entry box. Edit the main entry and customize the other settings as required

- Then click on **Mark.**

Creating the Index

After marking the entries, you can now follow the steps given below to create an index

- Click where you wish to add the index

- Go to the **Reference** tab, and click on the **Insert Index** button in the **Index group**

Index

- In the Index dialog box, set the following options

  - **Type**: This allows you to choose **Run-in** if you want subentries and sub-subentries to run together, and choose **Indented** to indent subentries and sub subentries below main entries.

  - **Columns:** This allows you to choose the number of columns

  - **Language:** With this option, you can choose a language for your table.

  - **Right Align Page Numbers:** This option allows you to right-align the entries so that the entries line up under one another.

  - **Tab Leader**: With this option, you can place a leader between the entry and the page number.

  - **Format:** This gives you access to nice and professional index layouts.

  - **Modify:** This option allows you to create an index style that suits your need.

- When you are done, click on **OK**

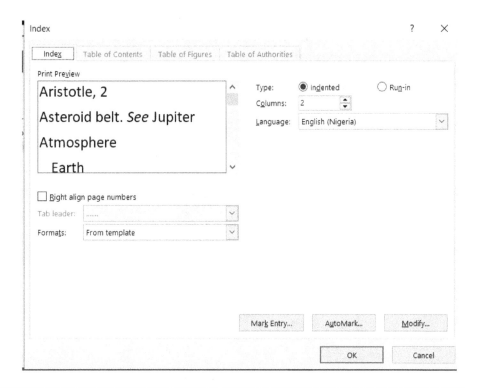

Editing the Index

Before you edit the index in your document, the Index field marker must be visible. The Index field markers are enclosed in curly brackets with the letter XE and the text of the index entry in quotation mark E.g. **{: XE:" Word"}**

To edit an index

- Click on **Show/Hide ¶** button in the Paragraph group on **the Home tab**

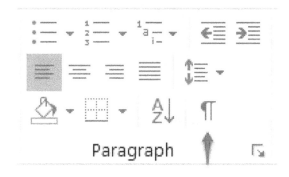

- Find the XE field for the entry you wish to change and change the text inside the quotation mark

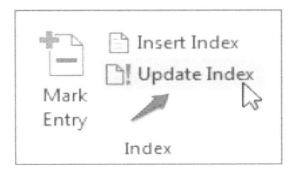

- To update the index, go to the **Reference** tab and click on **Update Index** in the **Index** group.

Note: To delete an index entry, select the entire entry field, and then press the **DELETE** key

Putting Footnotes and Endnotes in Your Documents

A **Footnote** in a document adds a note, comments, or reference the usually appears at the bottom of a page in a document, and it is represented by a number or symbol in a text.

An **Endnote** also adds notes, comments, or references but appears at the end of a section, chapter, or document, and it is also represented by a number or symbol in a text.

Inserting a Footnote

To add a footnote to your document, follow the steps below

- Place the insertion point where you wish to add a footnote

- Go to the **Reference** tab and click on **Insert Footnote**

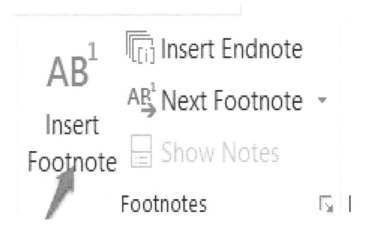

- A reference mark is inserted where the footnote mark is added at the bottom of the page.

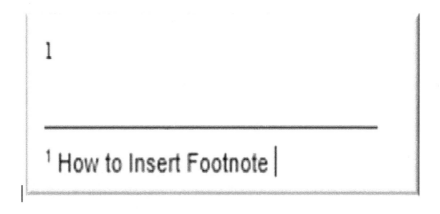

Inserting an Endnote

To add an endnote to your document, follow the steps below

- Place the insertion point where you wish to add an endnote

- Go to the **Reference** tab and click on **Insert Endnote**

- A reference mark is inserted where the endnote mark is added at the bottom of the document

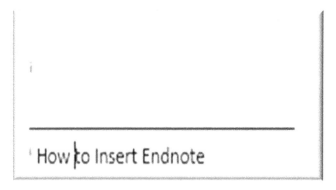

How to Insert Endnote

Customizing the Footnotes and Endnotes

After you must have added your footnotes and endnotes to your document, you can change the way they appear. For instance, you can choose to change the number format of your footnote or endnote in your document. To do this, follow the steps given below

- Go to the **Reference** tab and click on the **Footnote** button

- In the **Footnote and Endnote** dialog box, set the following options to customize your footnote and endnote

  - **Footnotes**: select the Bottom of the page to place the footnote at the bottom of the page.

  - **Endnotes:** Select End of Document to place the endnotes at the back of the document. In case your document is in sections, select End of Section to make the endnote appear at the end of the section.

  - **Columns:** This allows you to choose the number of columns you want while running the footnotes and endnotes

  - **Number Format:** With this option, you can change the number format to A B C, I II III, or other numbering styles.

  - **Custom Mark**: This option allows you to mark a note with a symbol by clicking on the Symbol button.

- o **Start At:** This allows you to choose where you want the numbering of the notes to start from.

- o **Numbering**: This option allows you to number your notes by selecting Continuous or Restart Each Section.

Editing, Moving and Deleting Footnotes or Endnotes

- **Editing**: To edit a footnote or endnote, double click on the number or symbol in the footnote or endnote. Then start editing.

- **Moving:** To move a footnote or endnote, select the number or symbol, and drag to the new location. You can cut and paste it to a new location.

- **Deleting:** To delete a footnote or endnote, select the number or symbol, and press the **Delete** key.

CHAPTER TWELVE

SHORTCUT KEYS IN WORD 365

The shortcut keys are the combination of two or more keys to carry out a command. Rather than going through a long process of executing a task, the shortcut keys provide an easy and fast method to get it done. Now, we will be going through some shortcut keys that can be found in Word 365.

Frequently Used Shortcuts

Shortcut Keys	Functions
Ctrl + A	To select or highlight all content of a document.
Ctrl + B	To apply the bold formatting to text
Ctrl + O	To open a document.
Ctrl + N	To open or create a new document.
Ctrl + S	To save a document.
Ctrl + X	To cut the part of the content selected in a document.
Ctrl + W	To close the document.
Ctrl + C	To copy the selected content of a document to the Clipboard.
Ctrl + V	To paste the content of a document from the Clipboard
Ctrl + I	To apply the italic formatting text

Ctrl + U	To apply the underline formatting text
Ctrl +]	To decrease the font size by 1 point.
Ctrl + [	To increase the font size by 1 point.
Ctrl + E	To align the text to the center
Ctrl + L	To align the text to the left
Ctrl + R	To align text to the right
Ctrl + Z	To undo an action
Ctrl + Y	To repeat or redo an action
Esc	To cancel a command
Ctrl + Alt + S	To split the document window
Alt + Shift + C or Ctrl + Alt + S	To remove the document window split.

Ribbon Keyboard Shortcuts

Shortcut keys	Functions
Alt + Q and enter the search term	To move to the Tell me or Search field on the Ribbon to search for assistance or Help content.
Alt + F	To open the Backstage view of the File tab
Alt + H	To open the Home tab
Alt + N	To open the Insert tab
Alt + G	To open the Design tab

Alt + P	To open the Layout tab
Alt + S	To open the Reference tab
Alt + M	To open the Mailing tab
Alt + R	To open the Review tab
Alt + W	To open the View tab
Alt or F10	To select an active tab on the ribbon, and activate the access key
Shift + Tab or Tab Key	To move the focus to commands on the ribbon
Ctrl + Left or Right arrow key	To move between command groupings on the ribbon.
Arrow Keys	To move among the items on the ribbon
Spacebar or Enter	To activate the selected button
Down Arrow key	To open the list for the selected command
Alt + Down Arrow Key	To open the menu for the selected button.
Down Arrow Key	To move to the next command when a menu or submenu is open.
Ctrl + F1	To expand or collapse the ribbon.
Shift + F10	To open the context menu
Left Arrow Keys	To move to the submenu when the main menu is open or selected.

Navigating the Document Keyboard Shortcuts

Shortcut Keys	Keys
Ctrl + Left Arrow Key	To move the cursor one word to the left.
Ctrl + Right Arrow Key	To move the cursor one word to the right.
Ctrl + Up Arrow Key	To move the cursor up by one paragraph
Ctrl+ Down Arrow Key.	To move the cursor down by one paragraph.
End	To move the cursor to the end of the current line.
Home	To move the cursor to the beginning of the current line.
Ctrl +Alt +Page Up	To move the cursor to the top of the screen
Ctrl +Alt +Page Down	To move the cursor to the bottom of the screen.
Page Up	To move the cursor by scrolling the document view up by one screen.
Page Down	To move the cursor by scrolling the document view down by one screen.
Ctrl +Page Down	To move the cursor to the top of the next page.
Ctrl + Page Up	To move the cursor to the top of the previous page.

Ctrl + End	To move the cursor to the end of the document.
Ctrl + Home	To move the cursor to the beginning of the document.
Shift + F5	To move the cursor to the location of the previous revision.
Ctrl + F	To display the Navigation task pane, to search within the document content.
Ctrl + G	To display the Go To dialog.
Ctrl + Alt + Z	To move through the locations of the four previous changes made to the document.

Preview and Print Document Keyboard Shortcuts

Shortcut Keys	Functions
Ctrl + P	To print the document.
Ctrl + Alt + I	To switch to the print preview
Arrow Keys	To move around the preview page when zoomed in
Page Up o Page Down	To move by one preview page when zoomed out.
Ctrl + Home	To move to the first preview page when zoomed out.
Ctrl + End	To move to the last preview page when zoomed.

Select Text and Graphics Keyboard Shortcuts

Shortcut Keys	Functions
Shift + Arrow Keys	To select text
Ctrl + Shift + Left Arrow Key	To select the word to the left
Ctrl + Shift + Right Arrow Key	To select the word to the right.
Shift + Home	To select from the current position to the beginning of the current line.
Shift + End	To select from the current position to the end of the current line.
Ctrl + Shift + Up Arrow Key	To select from the current position to the beginning of the current paragraph
Ctrl + Shift + Down Arrow Key	To select from the current position to the end of the current paragraph.
Shift + Page Up	To select from the current position to the top of the screen.
Shift + Page Down	To select from the current position to the beginning of the document.
Ctrl +Shift + Home	To select from the current position to the beginning of the document.
Ctrl + Shift + End	To select from the current position to the end of the document.

| Ctrl + Alt + Shift + Page Down | To select from the current position to the bottom of the window. |

Edit Text and Graphics Keyboard Shortcuts

Shortcut Keys	Functions
Ctrl + Backspace	To delete one word to the left
Ctrl + Delete	To delete one word to the right.
Ctrl + X	To cut the selected content to the Clipboard
Ctrl + V	To paste the content of the Clipboard
Alt + F3	To define an Auto Text block with the content selected.
Ctrl + F3	To cut the selected to the Spike
Ctrl + Shift + F3	To paste the content of the Spike.
Ctrl + Shift + C	To copy the selected formatting.
Ctrl + Shift + V	To paste the selected formatting.
Alt + Shift + R	To copy the header or footer used in the previous section of the document.
Ctrl + H	To display the Replace dialog
Alt + N, M	To insert a SmartArt graphic
Alt + N, W	To insert a WordArt graphic

Align and Format Paragraph Keyboard Shortcuts

Shortcut Keys	Functions
Ctrl + E	To align the paragraph to the center
Ctrl + J	To justify the paragraph
Ctrl + L	To align the paragraph to the left
Ctrl + R	To align the paragraph to the right.
Ctrl + M	To indent the paragraph
Ctrl + T	To create a hanging indent.
Ctrl + Shift+ T	To remove a hanging indent.
Ctrl + Q	To remove the paragraph formatting
Ctrl + 1	To apply single spacing to the paragraph
Ctrl + 2	To apply double spacing to the paragraph
Ctrl + 0 (Zero)	To remove or add space before the paragraph
Ctrl + Alt + 1	To apply the Heading 1 style
Ctrl + Alt + 2	To apply the Heading 2 style
Ctrl + Alt + 3	To apply the Heading 3 style
Ctrl + Shift + N	To apply the Normal style

| Ctrl + Shift + S | To display the Apply Style task pane |
| Ctrl + Alt + Shift + S | To display the Style task pane |

Format Characters Keyboard Shortcuts

Shortcut Keys	Functions
Ctrl + Shift + K	To apply small caps formatting
Ctrl + Equal Sign (=)	To apply the subscript formatting
Ctrl + Shift + Plus Sign (+)	To apply the superscript formatting
Ctrl + Spacebar	To remove manual character formatting.
Ctrl + Shift + Q	To change the selected text to a Symbol font.

Keyboard Shortcuts to Review a Document

Shortcut Keys	Functions
Ctrl + Alt + M	To insert a comment
Ctrl + Shift + E	To turn on or off the Change Track
Alt + Shift + C	To close the Reviewing Pane

Keyboard Shortcuts for Switching the Document View

Shortcut Keys	Functions
Alt + W, F	To switch to the Read Mode view
Ctrl + Alt + P	To switch to the Print Layout view
Ctrl + Alt + O	To switch to the Outline view
Ctrl + Alt + N	To switch to the Draft view.

The Function Keys

Shortcut keys	Functions
F1	Go to Get Help or visit Microsoft Office Online.
F2	To move text or graphics.
F3	To insert AutoText
F4	To repeat the last action.
F5	To open Go To command
F6	To go to the next pane or frame
F7	To open the Spelling command
F8	To extend a selection
F9	To update selected fields
F10	To activate the menu bar
F11	Go to the next field.
F12	To open the Save As command

Ctrl + Function Keys

Shortcut Keys	Functions
Ctrl + F2	To open the Print Preview command
Ctrl + F3	To cut to the spike
Ctrl + F4	To close the Window
Ctrl + F5	To restore the document window size.
Ctrl + F6	To move to the next window
Ctrl + F7	To open the Move command.
Ctrl + F8	To open the Size command
Ctrl + F9	To insert an empty field
Ctrl + F10	To maximize the document window.
Ctrl + F11	To lock a field.
Ctrl + F12	To open the Open command

Shift + Function Key

Shortcut Keys	Functions
Shift + F1	To start context-sensitive Help or reveal formatting.
Shift + F2	To copy text
Shift + F3	To change the case of letters
Shift + F4	To repeat a Find or Go To action.

Shift + F5	To move to the last change
Shift + F6	To move to the previous pane or frame
Shift + F7	To open the Thesaurus command.
Shift + F8	To shrink a selection.
Shift + F9	To switch between a field code and its result.
Shift + F10	To display the shortcut menu.
Shift + F11	To move to the previous field.
Shift + F12	To open the Save command.

Alt + Function Key

Shortcut Keys	Functions
Alt + F1	To go to the next field.
Alt + F3	To create an Auto Text entry.
Alt + F4	To close Microsoft Word.
Alt + F5	To restore the program window size
Alt + F7	To find the next misspelling or grammatical error
Alt + F8	To run a macro
Alt + F9	To switch between all field codes and their results.
Alt + F10	To maximize the program window

Alt + F11	To display the Microsoft Visual Basic code.

CHAPTER THIRTEEN

TIPS AND TRICKS ON WORD 365

I know the journey from chapter one up to the last chapter of this book has not been easy. However, to compensate you for enduring this long, I will be teaching some tips and tricks that will surely come in handy in the course of using Word 365.

Now let's check out these tips and tricks

Saving Word File as a PDF

PDF, an acronym for **Portable Document File** is a file created to be displayed and printed in a Web browser and Adobe Acrobat Reader.

To save a word file as a PDF, follow the steps given below

- Go to the **File** tab and click on **Export** to open the **Export** window

- Click on **Create a PDF/XPS** button

- In the **Publish as PDF or XPS** dialog box appears, enter the name of the file and the location where you want to save the file.

- Then click on the **Publish** button

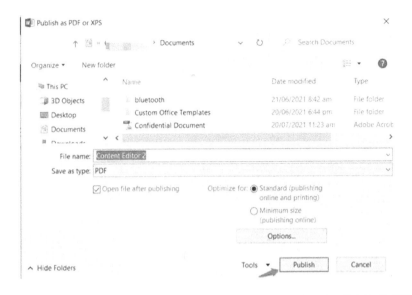

Changing Word File into a Web Page

To change a Word file into a web page, follow the steps given below

- Go to the **File** tab and click on **Export** to open the **Export** window

- Click on **the Change File Type** button

- In the **Change File Type** options that appear, select **Single File Web Page**

- In the **Save As** dialog box that appears, click on the **Change Title** button, and enter the title that will be displayed in the title bar of the browser in the **Enter Text** dialog box. Then click on **Ok.**

- Select a folder to save your new web page, and then click on the **Save** button

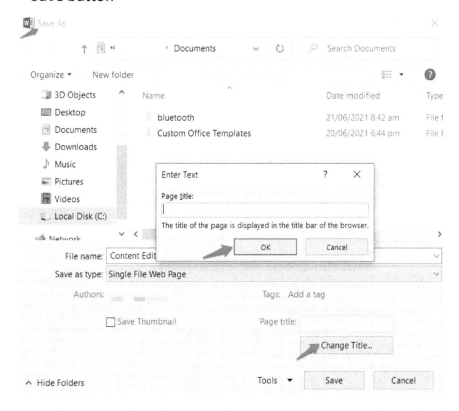

Customizing Keyboard Shortcuts in Words

A keyboard shortcut is a combination of keys that are assigned to carry out a command or an action. These shortcut keys can also be assigned to symbols, macros, fonts, styles, and building blocks. Examples of keyboard shortcuts are Ctrl + S, F6, Shift + Alt, etc.

To customize the keyboard shortcuts, follow the steps provided below:

- Go to the **File** tab, click on **Options,** and select **Customize Ribbon**

- In the **Customize the Ribbon and keyboard shortcut** pane, move the mouse to the bottom and click on **Customize.**

- In the Customize Keyboard dialog box, set the following options

  o **Categories Box**: In the Category box, select the category that contains the command or item you wish to assign a keyboard shortcut to.

  o **Command Box**: In the Command box, choose the name of the command or other item you intend to assign a keyboard shortcut to.

  o **Current Keys Box:** This contains the keyboard shortcut that is currently to a command or other item.

  o **Press New Shortcut Key Box:** This is where you enter the keys combination you want to assign to a command or item. For instance, press **CTRL** with the key you wish to use.

  o **Save Changes Box**: This box allows you to select the current document name or template you wish to save the keyboard shortcut changes in.

- Then click on the **Assign button** and assign the new keyboard shortcut.

- To remove a keyboard shortcut, go to the **Current keys** box, select the keyboard shortcut that you want to remove, and click on **Remove**

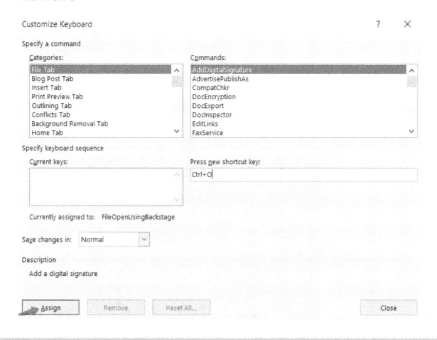

Customizing the Status Bar

The status bar is located at the bottom of the window. op

You can choose what appears on the status by right-clicking the status bar. Here you get to see a drop-down list where you can select and deselect items to appear on the screen.

Changing the Screen Background of Your Word Environment

To change the background screen of your Word 365 interface, follow the steps given

- Go to the **File** tab and click on **Account**

- Go to the **Office Theme** and choose any option in the drop-down list.

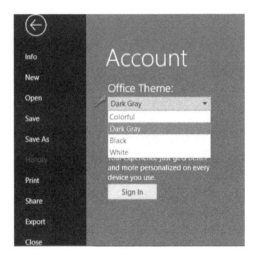

Locking a File with a Password

You can lock your file with a password to others from accessing your files. To password your file, follow the steps given below

- Go to the **File** tab and click on **Info**

- In the **Info** window, click on **Protect Document** button, and choose **Encrypt with Password** on the drop-down list.

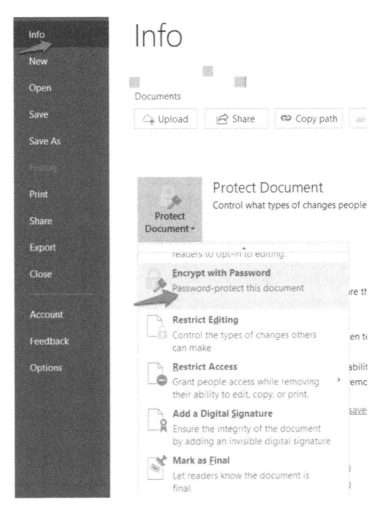

- In the **Encrypt** dialog box, input the password in the **Password** text box and then click on **Ok.**

- Enter the password again in the **Confirm Password** dialog box.

- Then click on **Ok**

Removing a Password from a File

To remove a password from a file, follow the steps given below

- Open the file you need to remove its password

- Go to the **File** tab and click on **Info**

- In the **Info** window, click on **Protect Document** button, and choose **Encrypt with Password** on the drop-down list

- In the **Encrypt** dialog box, delete the password, and click on **OK**

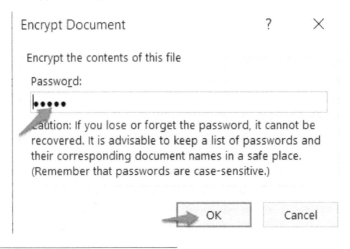

Renaming Tabs in Word 365

You can rename tabs such as the Home tab, Insert tab, Design tab to any name you desire by following the steps given below

- Right-click on the tab and select **Customize the Ribbon**

- In the **Word Options** dialog box, go to the **Customize Ribbon** category, and select the tab you wish to rename

- Click on the **Rename** button where the Rename dialog box will appear.

- Input the new name and click on **Ok**

Auto Update Date and Time

You can update the date and time in your document by following the steps given below

- Go to the **Insert** tab and click on the **Date & Time** button in the **Text** group

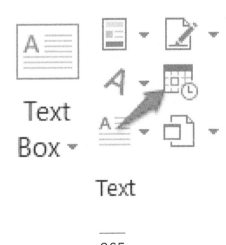

- In the **Date and Time** dialog box, select the date format you want and then click on the **Update Automatically** box in the bottom-right corner.

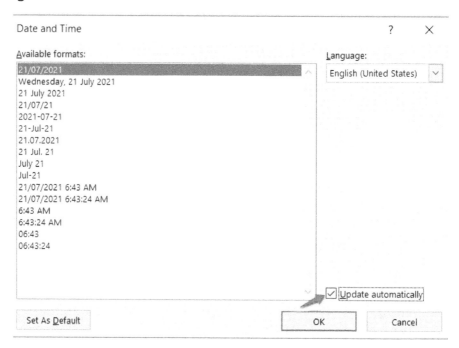

CONCLUSION

The journey of a thousand miles begins with a step!

If you are currently reading this part of this user guide, then I must congratulate you on a job well done. Truly, it has not been easy reading through each page of this book to get adequate knowledge of Word 365.

Reading this book is not just enough, ensure to practice what you have learned from time to time, and you will be amazed to see how far you will go with the knowledge gained from this user guide.

Looking forward to hearing from you soon.

INDEX

Update Table · 41, 43, 44, 233, 234
Uppercase · 83

V

View tab · 51, 61, 62, 64, 69, 93, 97, 246
View Tab · 51, 61

W

Watermark · 37, 208, 210, 211, 212, 213

Web Layout · 52, 61, 62, 70
Web Page · 258
Window · 13, 14, 53, 54, 254
word · 239
Wrap Text · 40
Wrapping · 40, 90, 157, 196

Z

Zoom · 53, 69